Anonymous

The English Charlemagne Romances

Vol. 4

Anonymous

The English Charlemagne Romances
Vol. 4

ISBN/EAN: 9783337345631

Printed in Europe, USA, Canada, Australia, Japan

Cover: Foto ©Thomas Meinert / pixelio.de

More available books at **www.hansebooks.com**

THE
ENGLISH CHARLEMAGNE ROMANCES.

PART III.

The Lyf of the Noble and Crysten Prynce,

Charles the Grete,

TRANSLATED FROM THE FRENCH BY WILLIAM CAXTON
AND PRINTED BY HIM 1485.

EDITED NOW FOR THE FIRST TIME, FROM THE UNIQUE COPY
IN THE BRITISH MUSEUM,

with Introduction, Notes, and Glossary,

BY

SIDNEY J. H. HERRTAGE, B.A.,

EDITOR OF "GESTA ROMANORUM," "SIR FERUMBRAS," ETC.

LONDON:
PUBLISHED FOR THE EARLY ENGLISH TEXT SOCIETY,
BY N. TRÜBNER & CO., 57 & 59, LUDGATE HILL.
MDCCCLXXXI.

INTRODUCTION.

THE present volume, completing Part III. of the English Charlemagne Rómance series, requires but little introduction. I have already referred to it in my edition of *Sir Ferumbras*, Introd. pp. viii, ix. It contains the whole life of Charlemagne, with a brief sketch of the early kings of France, and includes all the incidents narrated in *Sir Ferumbras*, *The Sowdone of Babyloyne*, *Roland and Vernagu*, and the *Song of Roland*.

Caxton's "Lyf of the Noble and Crysten Prynce, Charles the Grete" survives only in the unique copy preserved in the British Museum (Press Mark c. 10, b. 9). It is a folio volume, containing 96 leaves, the signatures running from A ij to M viij, and is perfect, but without title-page. The colophon tells us that the "werke was fynysshed in the reducyng of hit in to Englysshe the xviij day of Juyn, the seconde yere of kyng Rychard the thyrd, and the yere of our lord MCCCCLXXXV, and enprynted the fyrst day of decembre the same of our lord, & the fyrst yere of kyng Harry the seuenth."

The type is that classed by Mr. Blades as 4*. The pages have two columns, each containing 39 lines, and each line measuring $2\frac{3}{8}$ inches. There are neither folios nor catchwords. The initial woodcut letters are 3 lines deep.

In 1743 the volume was sold by R. Harley to Osborne the bookseller, the price not mentioned. In 1773 it became the property of J. Ratcliffe at a cost of £13, and in 1776 it was sold by him to George III for £4. 4. 0.

As Caxton himself tells us, the work here reprinted is a translation of the French prose romance of Fierabras, itself a compilation

partly from the *Speculum Historiale* of Vincent de Beauvais, and
partly from the old French romance of Fierabras. The exploits of
Charlemagne were related in numerous histories and romances, both
in French and Latin, in prose and in verse, as early as the 12th and
13th centuries. From the envoy of the anonymous author of the
original French version we learn how Henry Bolomyer, a canon of
Lausanne, induced him to gather together into one connected narra-
tive these disjointed fragments. A comparison of his work with that
of Vincent of Beauvais shows clearly that his researches were by no
means confined to the *Speculum Historiale*. I have already given a
short account of the original French work.[1] One version in the
Grenville Library, 10531, is doubly unique, being not only the only
copy of that particular version known to be in existence, but also
the only production of the press of Symon du Jardin, at Geneva,
which has come down to us. Brunet had heard of it, but doubted
its existence (*Suppl.* II. p. 231). It is undated and without signatures, pagination, or illustrations.

A second version of the original French is also preserved in the
same library, No. 10532. It also is a folio volume of 65 leaves,
signatures running from A j to L v. On L v *b* is a woodcut similar
to that at the end of the copy already described. This also is
unique, and has the following colophon : "Cy finist Fierabras imprime
a lyon lan de grace mil qualtre cens quatre vingtz et seize. Le xx
iour de nouembre." There are numerous woodcuts throughout the
work, evidently copied from the same source as those in the Royal
Fierabras described below, but much coarser and plainer. They are
also frequently reversed, and, as in the royal copy, the same woodcut
is at times made to serve for two or more incidents of a similar
character.

In the library of the late Mr. Huth is a version, undated, in folio,
black letter, with woodcuts, and the colophon : "Cy finist Fierabras.
Imprime a lyon par maistre Guillaume le roy. Le cincquiesme Jour
du moys de Juilliet. Deo gracias." It contains 108 leaves, and is
the copy described by Brunet. It appears to have belonged originally

---

[1] Introd. to *Sir Ferumbras*, pp. vi, vii.

to the library of the Academy at Lyons. In the same library is a version in German containing 53 leaves, of which another copy is in the British Museum.[1]

The copy of the French *Fierabras* which I have used for comparison with the English translation, is that preserved in the Royal Library (Press mark, C. 6, b. 12). It is a folio volume of 115 leaves, without title-page. Woodcuts are freely introduced. On the back of sign. A i. is a large one representing Fierabras on horseback, and another on O 5 representing Charlemagne on his throne, and surrounded by his douzeperes. The preface begins on A ij, the index on A ij *b*, and the text on A vj. The colophon runs: " Cy finist Fierabras. Imprime a genesue Par maistre Loys Garbin bourgois de la dicte cite. Lan mil cccc. lxxxiij. et Le xiij iour de moys de Mais. Deo gracias. Amen." The woodcuts are in many cases most comical: perhaps the most ludicrous are those which are intended to represent Floripas killing Britamont, and Richard swimming the torrent of Flagot. In one in which the sacred relics are shown, only three nails appear, and in two others the Saracens are represented as bombarding the tower of Aigremont with cannons.

In a few instances the same cut is employed to represent two incidents of a similar character. Thus that representing Oliver before Balan is also used for Guy before the Sultan.

In his translation, Caxton has followed his original so closely and even slavishly, that at times it is difficult, if not impossible, to understand his meaning without a reference to the language of the original. Frequently he has used the very words of the French author, and still more frequently he has merely given them an English dress. Caxton probably is responsible for the introduction of more French words into our language than any other writer.

In his epilogue Caxton tells us that he undertook the rendering into English of this Lyf of Charles the Grete at the instigation of " a good and synguler frend, Maister wylliam daubeny, one of the tresirers of the Iewellys of the noble and moost crysten kyng', our naturel and soucrayn lord late of noble memorye kyng Edward the fourth." I have endeavoured to identify this Sir William Daubeny,

---

[1] See *Sir Ferumbras*, Introd. p. vii.

and to ascertain the nature of the duties pertaining to his office as
keeper of the jewels. As to the latter—

The copy of the *Liber Niger Domus Regis Anglie*, believed to be
that of Edward IV. in the Harleian MS 642, has the following
section on leaf 49, &c. on the Keeper of the Jewels, his clerk,
yoman, groom, chariot, &c.

Office of Jewelhouse

hath an Architector callid Clarke of the Kinges or keeper of Joyalx,
or Theasaurer of the Chambre: this officer taketh bui Indenture
betwixt him and the Kinge, all that he findes in his office of gold,
siluer, pretious stones, and the mark*es* of euery thinge. Alsoe he
receaueth the yearely guift*es* by Record of the Chamberlaine. Item
he receaueth by Indenture of the Thesaurer of England, And by
ouersight of the Chamberlaine sitting in the Kingis Chambre or in
the hall with a *p*erson of like seruice, And for his Chambre at night
dimid*ium* cheate loafe, one quart wyne, one gallon of ale; And for
winter Liuerey, one perche de wax, one candle wax, two candels p*ar*is,
one dimid*ium* tallwood, and p*re*sent in Court vij^d. ob. [*leaf* 49 *back*].
In Checkerrolle and cloathing with howsold for winter and som*m*er,
or of the Countinghouse xl:^{s}. : his Liuerey is as Knight*es*, and if he be
sicke, he taketh in eating daies like the Squires for the bodie when
they bin lett blood or sicke, &c.   Also in this offise is a clarke vnder
him in the hall eatinge, taking for his liuerey at night, dimid*ium*
gallon ale, one candle p*ar*is, dimid*ium* tallwood, shide and cloathing
by the Countinghouse, or yerely twentie shilling*es*.   And if he be
sike, he taketh for all day one loafe of bread, one messe of gret
meate, dimid*ium* gallon ale.   And for this office a yoman eating in
the hall with yomen of Chambre, taking for his wages in the
Countinghouse, if he be p*re*sent, allowed by the Checkerrolle,
threepence ; And cloathing with the housold winter and sum*m*er for
chances and all other part, or eighteene shilling*es*, besides his reward
of the Jewelhouse for sure and diligent keeping of the King*es*
Joalxe yerely &c*t*.   And if he be sicke, he taketh such Liuerey as
doth the Clerke.   Also in this office a groome eating dayly in the
office, taking for his liuerey one loafe, one messe of grete meate,
dimidium gallon ale : And he setteth in the Liueries [*leaf* 50].   For
this office in season, one candle wax, two candles p*ar*is, one tallwood
dimid*ium*, And Rushes and litter for this office all the yeare of the
Sergeant Vsher of hall and Chambre.   Also this groome fetting
nightly for this office one gallon of ale : he helpeth to trusse and
beare to the Charriott, and awaiteth thervpon the safeguard ; and the
yoman also to attend vpon this carriage.   And this office hath also
lodgeing in the Countrie towne for all these horses and seruant*es*

suffisauntly by the herbergier. And the chiefe of this office The maister to haue into this Court two waiters, and the Clerke one two seruants, the Clerke honest seruant. The remenant goo to theire lodgeing in one seruant. the Countrey. And the yoman and groome haue one seruant. And for this office is assigned a Charriott with seauen horses and A Charriot with seauen all there apparell, horse-meate, shooeing, and the yomen and horses. groomis wagis therfore, foundyn of the charge of Thesaurer of housold to carrie the stuff of the Kinges in this office, and none other mans, by the ouersight of the Controller, betwixt the Thesaurer of housold, and this officer, be many interchaunges of siluer vessell, hoole and brooke, receaued or deliuered by officers by Indentures &c. As it will appeare in [*leaf* 50, *back*] The Accompt of housold. And as for othir thinges touching this office, behold in the title *De Oblationibus*[1] *Regis* capitulid before. all thinges of this office inward or outward, cometh and goeth by the knowledge of the Kinge, and by the Chamberlaines Record. Also if any Knight or Squire presume to weare the Kinges liuerey, but if he come ther by authoritie, or ellys by record in this office./

Thanks to the kindness of Mr. Selby of H.M. Record Office and Mr. Furnivall, I have been enabled to identify Sir W. Daubeny, and to give some interesting particulars relating to him. We first meet with his name in 1480-1, when he was appointed Searcher in the Port of London.[2] The substance of the Patent Roll is as follows :

[1] Vide de hoc antea : folio. 15. *b*. [On Gifts by the King in charity, &c.]

[2] The following note is derived from a bundle of Searchers' Accounts for the period :—

[*Ancient Miscellanea*. (Exch. Q. R.) Searchers' Accounts. Bundle 692. J. P. R. 2110.]

1—6 } London.—Account by John Lyn who was appointed by Hen. VII } letters patent dated 22 Sept. 1 Hen. VII. Searcher in the port of London, to wit, from 22 Sept. / to Mich. 6 Hen. VII., William Dawbeney late Searcher. / membrane.

This Account extending over five years and 8 days gives the sum received as *nil*.

This record states the duties to be—"ad explorandum per se in propria persona sua, et non per substitutum, omnes naves et batellas extra regnum Anglie transeuntes, et ad idem regnum venientes in portubus et locis predictis [*i. e.* in portu Civitatis Londonie], et ad scrutinium faciendum de omnibus navibus et batellis hujusmodi, et de personis de quibus sinistra suspicio haberi poterit, quod lane, pelles lanute, coria, panni, aut mercimonia custumabilia non cokettata nec custumata in eisdem navibus, aut aurum vel argentum in pecunia numerata, aut masa vel plata seu focalia carcata seu posita fuerunt ; vel si alique persone bullas litteras instrumenta vel processus vel aliqua alia Regi vel suditis Regis prejudicialia infra vel extra regnum Regis predictum, detuleri contra proclamaciones et inhibuciones ex parte Regis inde factas, Habendum et occupandum officium predictum quamdiu Regi placuerit, una cum medietate forisfacture predicte."

9 Novr, 20 Edw. IV, 1480. Memb. 21. Appointment of Wm.
Daubeny as Searcher in the Port of London & other places adjoin-
ing the same, with the usual fees & emoluments, & also the half
of all forfeit, was seized to the King's use. His substitute or substi-
tutes may act for him.

About the same time in a "Roll of Accounts, Michaelmas, 20
Edw. IV," there is an entry that John Barker of London, Goldsmith,
had received 100*l* from *William Daubeney* in part payment of 80
butts of malmsey purchased by him for the use of the King's
army.[1]

In 1483-4 he was re-appointed to the office of Searcher of the
Port to Richard III. In the Patent Roll his previous appointment
to the same office under Edward V. is referred to, and he is further
described as Clerk of the Jewels. In the Calr. of the Patent Rolls,
Ric. III. Appx. to 9th Report of Deputy Keeper of Records, p. 34,
the following particulars relating to Sir W. Daubeny are given :

1 Ric. III., p. 2, 1483-4. Membrane 20 (4) 16 Dec. Appointment of *William Daubeny*, clerk of the jewels, as searcher in
the port of London, with a grant of half of all the forfeitures, in
as full a manner as William Merston, esq. enjoyed the same :
which office the said *William Daubeney* fills by virtue of a patent
of Edward V. the bastard [entry 39], *ib.* p. 39, Membrance
7 (19).

11 Mar. Release to *William Daubeney* (or Dabeney), searcher in
the port of London, of all arrears of accounts, &c. to 6 March
last [entry 133].

ib. p. 42, Membrane 2 (24).

8 April. Appointment of John Wode, knt, Treasurer of England,
Robert Brakenbury, Constable of the Tower of London, Master
William Lacy, Master *William Dawbney*, and Master *Robert
Rydon*, as Commissaries General in the office of the Admiralty in
England. . .

ib. p. 67, Memb. 17 (9). 1 Ric. III, p. 4, 1483-4.

24 April. Grant to William Dawbeney, clerk of the jewels to
Edward IV., of an annuity of 10*l.* out of a farm in Watford
(Northampton), (2) by the hands of Eustace of Burneby and
Matill his wife, to hold the same until the gift, for life, of an
office of 20*l* yearly value ; further grant in survivorship to the

[1] Exchequer Issue Roll, Hen. III. to Edw. VI, ed. F. Devon, Appendix,
p. 500.

said *William Dawbeney* and Joan his wife of an annuity of 20 marks, the former patents of 22 June, 21 Edw. IV. (p. 2, m. 12), and 1 May,[1] 21 Edw. IV. (p. 1, m. 6), granting to them the said annuities, having been surrendered.

An order under the Privy Seal of Henry VII. in 1485 to the Treasurer and Chamberlaine of his Exchequer orders them to allow to his "beloved cousin John, arl of Oxenford," the sums of 100 marks and 100.£ out of his purchase-money of 800 marks for the manors of the late Wm. Alyngton during his son's minority, and the marriage of this son: This, because the Earl had paid 100 marks to Rich. Gardyner, alderman of London, "for so moche money by the said Richard Gardyner late lent unto Richard, duc of Gloucester, late, in dede and not of righte, kind of England, upon pledge of a salt of gold with a cover. . . the which salt . . . was delivered unto the said Richard Gardynere by one, *William Daubeney, knight, keeper of the juelx with the foresaid pretensed king* . . . and also the summe of c. li. parcell of xxiiij ͨ. li by the said late pretensed king borowed of the maire and aldermen of our said citie of London . . . and for suertie and contentaciom of the said xxiiij ͨ. li. the said late pretensed king laide in plege to the said maire and aldermen a coronalle gold garnished with many other grete and riche juelx, as by a bille endented betwix the said maire and aldremen, on that one partie, and the foresaid William Daubeney, then keper of juelx of the said pretensed king on that othre partie thero made, more plainly doth appere.[2]

In Sept. 1484 we find the following orders: "Parcelles of clothing [&c.] to be delivered by the said bishop to the said erle [of Desmond]. . . . Item, a nother lettre direct to Mr. *William Dawbeney*, clerk of the kinges juelles, to delivere unto the said bisshop for the said erle of Dissemond, a coler of gold of xx ͭ ͥ oz., xxx ͭ ͥ li.—Letters and Papers t. Rich. III. & Hen. VI, ed. Gairdner, Rolls Series, 1861, p. 713.

There is no William Daubeny's will of Caxton's time at the Probate Office, but the following items culled from various sources appear to refer to Caxton's friend, and his family:

Dame Joan Dawbeny, wife of Sir Wm. Dawbeny, was buried at the Augustine Friers Church, Broadstreet Ward, London, [no date given].[3] John, son and heir of Sir Giles Dawbeny, is buried in the same church.

[1] 1 March: in the patent roll of 21 Edw. IV.
[2] *Memorials Illustrative of the Reign of Henry VII*, p. 214. (Rolls Series.)
[3] Stowe's *Surray of London*, 1633, p. 186, col. 2.

Sir Wm. Stanley, William Dawbeney late of London, gentleman, & others were attainted of treason for rebelling against Henry VII. Act of Attainder in the *Rolls of Parliament*, vol. 6, p. 503.

Mr. Walter Rye says that this may be the same man as Sir William, because, in an official document like the above, the title of Knight conferred by the usurper, Rich. III, would probably not be acknowledged. (But compare the order under the Privy Seal in 1485, on the preceding page.)

Mr. Rye also thinks our Wm. D. was connected with the Norfolk Dawbeneys. In Blomfield's *Norfolk*, Wm. Dawbeney, of North Burlingham, after 1428 bought a property which his grandson Thomas sold in 1528. *10*

The Series of English Charlemagne Romances will be completed by the issue next year of the romances of *Roland and Vernagu* and *Sir Otuel*, from the Auchinleck MS., and the curious poem of *Rauf Coilȝear* from the unique printed copy.

SIDNEY J. HERRTAGE.

Mill Hill, N.W., October 1881.

paynyms, and that was by the ayde of fyerabras, which
for loue of Charles dyd fyght, and made grete dyscomfyture of the sarasyns. for there he put to deth

4 Tempeste, and the olde Rubyon, and moo than fyfty
other of these mastyns myscreauntes. & he there bare
hym in suche wyse that there was not one persone that
durst come tofore hym to resyste hym.

Fierabras slays more than 50 Saracens.

8 ¶ How the peres of Fraunce whyche were in
the toure came oute whan they sawe the
hoost, & how thadmyral was taken &
holden prysonner : capitulo   xiiij

12 THe paynyms & frensshe men, alwaye perseuer-
yng in mortal batuylle, coude not make thende,
eche one of other, For the multytude of the paynyms was so grete that they my3t not be dyscomfyted.

16 Whan [1]the barons that were in the tour sawe the fayt,
& that they that kepte the toure were goon to the
socours and crye of thadmyral, they sprange out, & eche
took an hors of them þat were dede, which ranne at al

20 aduenture ; and eche also took his swerde in his hond,
& sodeynly cam vpon the sarasyns for to passe thurgh
them to the frensshe hoost, & made so grete bruyt that
the moost hardyest of the paynyms gaf them waye, &

24 lete them passe, and in especyal rolland, for where he
smote with durandal, cam neuer after tofore hym. & at
thys departyng was derly recomanded guy of bourgoyn
of florypes, for she had fere of hym. Neuertheles, whan

28 they were assembled wyth the other, wythoute letyng
them to be knowen, went vpon the sarasyns, & helde
them soo short that anone they slewe them in suche wyse
þat the other put them to flyght : for there was neuer

32 larke fledde more ferfully tofore þe sperhawke than the
sarasyns fledde tofore rolland. Thadmyral knewe wel

The French knights, seeing the battle, sally out, and seizing each a stray horse, (5533)

charge the Sara-cens, and force their way through them, (5512)

scattering them like larks before the hawk. (5550)

[1] k ij, col. 2.

hys destructyon by the comyng⸱ of the peres that were
in þᵉ toure, & cryed⸱ wyth an h[y]e voys : "mahon, my
god, to whome I haue gyuen my self, and⸱ haue doon to
so moche honour, thou hast forgoten[1] me ! Remembre 4
me now !   ¶ For and euer I may gete the, I shal bete the
bothe flankes, [2]hede & vysage, and⸱ also put out thyn eyen,
fals recreaunt god⸱ that thou art." he thus sayeng⸱, he
was so pursyewed⸱ and smyton that he fyl doun vnder 8
his hors, and was taken, and⸱ not slayn, at the request of
hys sone fyerabras, to thende that he shold be aduysed⸱
to byleue in Ihesu cryst, & in the holy Trynyte, &
bycome crysten, & al his controye. Thenne the bataylle 12
took an ende ; and⸱ he that wold⸱ not be conuerted⸱ was
incontynent put to deth. Somme fledde, and somme
were taken. Thenne after thys the Frensshe men
wente & vnarmed them, & Charles sawe there hys 16
barons whom he desyred so moche to see, & in especial
his neuew rolland, & Olyuer, whom he loued so moche,
& were so gretly valyaunt. It can not be sayd⸱ ne
expressed⸱ the Ioye that was emonge them ; & the con- 20
solacyon & reioycyng⸱ of kyng⸱ charles was Inestymable.
Thenne they recounted alle thynges what were happend⸱
to them, & of theyr daungers and⸱ Ieopardyes whiche
they had⸱ escaped⸱, & sorowes & lamentacions that they 24
had endured⸱, wherfore Charles and⸱ many other wept for
pyte. And⸱ thys endured⸱ many dayes, there where as
the hurt men & seek were heeled⸱, & they that were
hole passed theyr tyme in deduyte, tryumphe, and⸱ 28
Ioye.

[3]¶ How ballant, thadmyrall, for ony admony-
    cyon that was shewed' to hym, wold not
    be baptysed, and how after, guy of bour- 32
    goyn espoused florypes, & was crowned

---

[1] *orig.* forygoten.   [2] k ij, back.   [3] k ij, back, col. 2.

Balan invokes his
god Mahon (5569)

with threats.

He is unhorsed
and taken
prisoner, (5647)

and the battle
ends. (5681)

There is great
rejoicing over the
safety of the
knights. (5670)

The army rests
some days to
recruit their
strength.

kyng, and she quene of that contreye :
capitulo   XV

4   WHan charles had al appeased, he took ballant   Charles sends for
        the admyral tofore hys noblesse, & sayd to   Balan, (5719)
        hym in this maner : " ballant, al creatures
resonable owen to gyue synguler honour & pertyculer
louc to hym that hath gyuen to them beyng, knowleche,
8 & lyf, & it is wel requesyte & nedeful that he haue
honour and reuerence that hath made heuen and erthe,
& al that therein enhabyteth.   Wherfore by good ryght
he is superyour and abouen al ; And a grete abusyon   and, declaring the
12 is comprysed in hym which gyueth fayth and hope   idolatry,
in that whyche he hath made wyth hys hondes, & of   evil and folly of
mater dede, Insensyble, and that hath neyther reson
ne soule, as thy goddes dyabolyke, whyche may not
16 ne can gyue consolacyon to theyr subgettes.   Wher-
fore I warne the for the helthe of thy soule, and for the   calls on him to
preseruyng of thy body & of thy goodes, that thou   forsake it,
take awaye alle these Iniquytees and peruerse affectyons,
20 & byleue in the holy Trynyte, fader, sone, ¹and holy   and to believe in
ghoost, one onely god almyghty ; and byleue that the   God, (5721)
sone of god, for to repayre thoffence of our formest fader
adam, descended in to thys world, and took humanyte
24 in the wombe of the blessed vyrgyn marie, whyche was
al pure and wythoute spotte.   And byleue in the   and the articles of
artycles of the fayth, and obeye and kepe hys comande-   faith.
mentes, which he hath gyuen to vs for our helth.   and
28 byleue how he was taken of the Iewes, and by enuy   He recounts
hanged on the crosse for to redeme vs fro the paynes   ion, resurrection,
of helle.   Byleue hys resurrexyon and ascencyon in hys   and ascension,
body gloryfyed, and the other thynges, as the holy
32 baptesme whyche he hath establysshed, wyth the other   and says that if
sacramentes. & yf thou wylt thus byleue thou shalt   verted, nothing
be saued, & thou shalt neyther lose body ne goodes."   from him. (5722)

¹ k iij.

O 2

Balan swears he will never forsake Mahon. (5749)

Charles threatens him with death. (5756)

Fierabras intercedes for his father, who agrees to be baptised. (5783)

The font is prepared, (5789)

Thadmyral answerd that he wold no thynge do so, and sware that for deth ne for lyf he wold not leue Mahon. Themperour holdyng a naked swerd, sayd to hym, that yf he forsoke not Mahon he sħold do put ħym to deth. Fyerabras, seyng thys, kneled doun to therthe, & prayed hys fader to do as the emperour had sayd. Thadmyral fered the deth, & sayd that he was contente that the fonte sħold be blessed. Charles was glad, and dyd do make redy a fonte wyth [1]fayr water in a fayr vessel; and the bysshop wyth other mynystres of the chyrche dyd halowe the fonte, and made alle redy. & after, whan thadmyral was vncladde, the bysshop demaunded hym, sayeng: "Syr ballant, forsake ye mahon, and crye ye mercy to god of heuen for your trespacces? and byleue ye in Ihesu cryst, the sone of the vyrgyn marye?" whan thadmyral vnderstode these wordes, al hys body began to tremble. than, in despyte of

but Balan spits in it, and nearly kills the bishop, (5809)

who is saved by Ogier.

Ihesus, he spytte in the fonte, and caught the bysshoop, & wold haue drowned hym in the fonte, and had plonged hym therin, ne had not Ogyer haue been, whyche letted hym, & yet notwythstondyng, he gaf a grete stroke to thadmyral, that the blood came oute of ħys mouthe habondantly. Of thys were al abasshed that were present; and thenne the kyng sayd to Fyerabras: "ye be my specyal frende, Ye see that your fader wyl neuer be crystened, And also the oultrage that he hath doon to the fonte, it can not be excused but that he must be dede and dysmembred."

Fierabras again intercedes for Balan, (5813)

¶ Fyerabras requyred hym yet of a lytel pacyence, and yf he wold not amende hym, that thenne he sħold doo hys wylle.

¶ Florypes, the doughter of the Admyrall, seeyng thys, sayd:

but Floripas urges Charles to put him to death at once. (5819)

¶ "O Syr Emperour, wherfore [2]delaye ye so moche to put thys deuyl to deth? I retche not though

[1] k iij, col. 2. [2] k iij, back.

he be put to deth, so that I onely may haue guye
of bourgoyne to myn husbond, whom I haue so moche
desyred." Fyerabras answerd : "fayr suster, ye haue
4 grete wronge. For I ensure you, and swere by god
whiche hath made me, that I wold that I had lost
two of my membres, on the condycyon that he were a
good cristen man, & were baptysed and byleued in
8 Ihesu Cryst. ye wote wel that he is our fader whiche
hath engendred vs ; we ought to honour hym, and to
loue hys helth. ye are wel obstynat whan ye haue of
hym noo pyte." And after in wepyng sayd to his
12 fader : "O moost dyer fader, I praye you to be better
aduysed, and byleue in hym that hath fourmed you
to hys ymage, whyche is Ihesus, god souerayn, lyke as
themperour hath sayd ; and leue mahon, which hath
16 neither wytte ne reason, ne noo thyng is but gold &
stones, wherof he is composed. yf ye thus do, ye shal
do to vs grete Ioye, & of your enemyes ye shal make
frendes."

20   Ballant ansuerd : "fool & glouton that thou art,
speke nomore to me therof, thou art al oute of reson !
I shal neuer byleue in hym that deyed V. C. yere a-goon,
& acursed be he that putteth in hys byleue that he is
24 arysen fro deth [1] to lyf. by mahon, my god, yf I were
on my hors back, or I were taken, I shold angre charles,
that fool." whan fyerabras had al vnderstonden hym,
he said to charles that he shold do wyth hym hys
28 playsyr, "For by good ryght he ought to deye." Anon
themperour demanded who wold slee ballant, the vn-
mesurable felon. Thenne Ogier was present which
hated hym in his hert, & forthwyth he smote of hys
32 heed, & Fyerabras pardonned hym gladly. Thenne
after this, florypes sayd to Rolland that he shold
accomplysshe his promesses by-twene hyr and guy of
bourgoyn. rolland ansuerd : "ye say trouth," and
     [1] k iij, back, col. 2.

Fierabras re-
proves her for her
unfilial conduct,
(5823)

and implores his
father to consent
to be a Christian.
(5823)

Balan calls him a
fool, and declares
he will never do
so. (5843)

Charles asks who
will kill the
Sowdan. (5859)

Ogier volunteers,
and smites off his
head. (5865)

Roland reminds
Guy of his promise
to marry Floripas.
(5871)

Guy says he is
quite ready. (5875)

Floripas is
stripped to be
baptised. (5879)

All are struck by
her exceeding
beauty,

and especially
Charles. (5889)

She is baptised,

but her name is
not changed.
Guy and Floripas
are married,

and crowned king
and queen of
Spain. (5905)

after sayd to guye : ¶ " Syr, yo remembre wel what
wordes and loue hath been bytwene you & the
curtoys Florypes : kepe your trouth and promesse to
hyr." Guy ansuerd that he was redy to do al that 4
themperour wold haue hym to doo. Charles was
contente. Thenne anone afore theym allo she was
despoyled, and vnclad hyr for to be baptysed. She
beyng there al naked, shewed hyr beaute, whyche was 8
ryght whyte and wel formed, so playsaunt and amerouse
for the formosyte of hyr persone, that euery man
merueylled. ¶ For she had hyr eyen as clere as two
sterres, a fayre forhede and large, hyr nose ryght wel 12
stondyng in ¹the myddes of the vysage ; hyr chekes
were reed & whyt medled, hyr browes compaced as it
had been a lytel shadowe to the colour of the vysage ;
hyr heyr shynyng as golde, & that in soo good an ordre 16
accumyled that it henge bynethe hyr ²knees ; hyr mouth
was wel composed with an attemperat roundenes, a
smal longe necke, and hyr sholdres fayr & wel syttyng,
& ij pappes tofore, smale, rounde, & somwhat enhaunced 20
lyke ij rounde apples. And so wel was she made, and
so amerouse, that she smote the hertes of many, and
enflammed theyr entencyon wyth concupyscence, and
specyally of charles the Emperour, how wel that he was 24
auncyen & olde ; and in the fonte whyche was ordeyned
for the Admyral hyr fader, she was baptysed. And
charles & Duc thyery of ardayne were her godfaders,
wythout chaunchyng hyr name. And anone after, whan 28
she was honourably cladde, the bysshop wedded them,
& after, themperour comanded to brynge forth the crowne
of ballant, and crowned wyth-al guy of bourgoyn and
Florypes. And the bysshop sacred and blessed them. 32
And so tho said guy was kyng of that contreye, & gaf
a partye to Fyerabras, by condycion, that yf Fyerabras
wold haue it, he shold holde it of guye, and all ³that

¹ k iiij.   ² orig. kuees.   ³ k iiij, col. 2.

[1]euer guye sholdͤ haue, he sholdͤ holde it of charles.

After thys, the feest of the weddyngͭ andͤ espousaylles The wedding festivities last
enduredͤ viij dayes. And charles abode there two 8 days. (5913)
4 monethes andͤ two dayes, tyl that the contreye was wel
assuredͤ.

¶ How Florypes delyuerd the reliques to
themperour, and how they were prouedͤ'
8 by myracle, & of the retournyng' of
Charles, and of the ende of thys book.
[capitulo   xvj]

C Harles dyd suche dylygence in aygremore andͤ in
12   the contreye adiacent, that he that woldͤ not be
baptysed was put to deth, andͤ so serchedͤ oueral.
Andͤ on a sonday after masse he sente for florypes, andͤ
saydͤ to hyr: "fayr doughter, ye knowe how I haue Charles reminds Floripas of all he
16 crownedͤ you andͤ maadͤ you quene of thys contree. I haue had done for her, (5923)
accomplysshedͤ your desyre as to guye of bourgoyn,
your husbondͤ, Andͤ more ouer ye be baptysedͤ, and in
waye of sauacyon, and ye haue one of the valyauntest
20 body that is from hens in to Affryque. ¶ Andͤ he
andͤ fyerabras your broder shal haue thys regyon, Andͤ
I shal leue with hym xx M of my subgetes, to the
ende that the paynyms be alwaye in drede ; but ye and calls on her to produce the
24 haue not yet shewed [2]to me nothyngͭ of the holy sacred relics. (5931)
relyques that ye kepe." Florypes answerdͤ: "Syr
emperour, they shal be redy whan it pleseth you," and
thenne she brouȝt forth the chest in whyche they were Floripas brings him the coffer
28 honestly. containing them, (5936)

¶ Themperour knecledͤ doun on bothe hys knees, andͤ
enclyned bothe wyth hert & body, and bad the bysshop
to opene it, & shewe them, and so he dydͤ. And fyrst which Turpin reverently opens.
32 he shewedͤ the precyous crowne with whyche Ihesu
Cryst was crownedͤ wyth, whyche was of pryckyng

[1] *orig.* euer.   [2] k iiij, back.

The bishop takes out the holy crown of thorns, (5950)

thornes & of Ionques of the see. and wyth grete deuocyon it was shewed & adoured. And many there wepte
& wayled the deth of our lord Ihesu Cryst, and were
in grete deuocyon & contemplacyon. The bysshop, 4
which was deuoute & wyse, wold preue it, And lyfte it
vp on hye in the ayer, & wythdrewe hys hond, and the

which remains unsupported in the air,

crowne abode by itself in the ayer. & thenne the
bysshop certefyed to the [1]peple that was present, that 8
it was the crowne of Ihesu cryst, which he had on his
hede in the tyme of his passyon. Thenne euery man

emitting a delightful odour. (5954)

honoured it deuoutely ; & it had soo grete an odour
that eueryche meruaylled. and after, the bysshop took 12
the naylles by whyche god had hys handes[2] & feet

The other relics are proved in the same way.

perced, and preued them as he had proued the crowne
tofore, and semblably they abode [3]in the ayer myracu-

Charles thanks God for his mercies to him.

lously. And Charles, seyng al this, thanked humbly 16
God in sayeng : ¶ "O lord god eternal, whyche hast
gyuen to me grace that I haue surmounted myn enemyes Infydels, and hast put & sette me in the waye,
and gyuen conduyte to fynde your relyques whyche I 20
haue so longe desyred, I humbly rendre and gyue to
you thankes and praysynges. For now my contrey
may wel say that it shal be perpetuel honour to hit to
possede and haue thys precious tresour, whan it shal be 24
conteyned therin." The bysshop blessyd alle the

Turpin blesses the army with relics, and replaces them in the coffer.

people there in makyng the sygne of the crosse with
the said relyques, & after he sette them deuoutely ageyn
in their places. And the emperour dyd do sette them 28
on a ryche cloth of golde deuoutely. And whan they
were theron, the remenaunt that abode of them as smale

Charles's glove, in which is a small piece of relic,

pyeces, he took them deuoutely and put them in hys
gloue ; and after, he beyng in purpoos to retorne in to 32
hys contreye, he threwe the gloue to a knyght, but the
knyght took none hede & took it not ; & whan Charles
was a litel withdrawen he took hede of hys gloue, &

[1] *orig.* peyle.   [2] *orig.* haudes.   [3] k iiij, back, col. 2.

retorned and sawe hys gloue,—in whyche the said smale
pyeces of the sayd relyques were,—abode hangyng¹ in *remains miracul-*
ously suspended
thayer without susteynyng of ony thynge.   Thenne *in the air*
4 ¹ was this myracle seen euydently, and al thys was
shewed to the peple, For it abode in that maner whyles
they myght haue goon half a leghe.   And by this they *for an hour. (6002)*
were al reconformed to say that there was none abusyon
8 in byleuyng¹ & adouryng the sayd relyques.   And these
thynges tofore writon in this second book ben vnderstonden in the best partye & sygnyfycacion that I can
or wold say, And I haue not sayd ony thyng but that
12 I haue been wel enformed by writyng¹.   And as for the
book ensuyng, it shal make mencion of somme bataylles,
and of the ende of the barons of fraunce, of whome I
haue tofore spoken al alonge.

16 ¶ Here begynneth the iij book, whyche con- *The contents of*
the third book.
teyneth two partyes, by the chapytres
folowyng declared'.

¶ The fyrst partye of the thyrd book con-
20   teyneth xiiij chapytres, and speketh of the
warres made in spayne, and' of two meruayllous geauntes.

¶ How Saynt Iames appyered' to Charles,
24   and how, by the moyen and' the conduyte
of the sterres, he went in to galyce, &
what cytees he subdued : ca.   j

² Charles, the noble Emperour, after he had taken *Charles wishes*
after all his
28   moche payne for to mayntene the name of god *labours to rest*
from fighting,
for tenhaunce the crysten fayth, and to brynge al
the world in one trewe fayth and byleue, & that he
had goten many contrees, he purposed neuer more to

¹ k v.   ² k v. col 2.

and to devote
himself to
religion;

fyght ne to make bataylle, but to reste & lede forth a
contemplatyf lyf, in thankyng his maker of þᵉ grace
that he had gyuen to hym in surmountyng hys enemyes.
Neuertheles on a nyght it happed hym that he byhelde 4

but in a vision he
sees a line of
stars,

the heuen, & sawe a quantyte of sterres in ordre tendyng
alle the nyght one waye and one path. And they
began at the see of fryselond in passyng bytwene
alemayn and ytalye, bytwene Fraunce and guyanne, 8
And passed ryght the sayd sterres by gascoyne, basele,
Nauarre, and espayne, whyche contrees he had by hys
puyssaunce and contynuel payne conquerd and maad
crysten.   And after, the ende of the sayd sterres thus 12

pointing to
Galicia.

goyng in ordre, cam vnto galyce, where-as the body of
the holy appostle was, he nat knowyng the propre
place.   Euery nyght charles byhelde the waye of the
sayd sterres, and thought moche contynuelly what thys 16
myght be, & that it was not wythoute cause.   ¶ In
one nyght emonge the other that ¹charles thought on

A man appears to
him,

thys waye, a man appyered to hym in vysyon, whyche
was so fayr, so playsaunte, and so shynyng, that it was 20
meruaylle; whyche sayd to hym: "what doost thou,
my fayre sone?"   Charles, beyng al rauysshed, answerd:
"who arte thou, fayr syr?"   That other answerd: "I

who declares he
is St. James,
the Apostle of
Galicia,

am Iames, the appostle of Ihesu Cryst, the sone of 24
Zebedee, and propre broder of saynt Iohan the euangelyst, & am he whom god chaas to preche the crysten
fayth and hys doctryne in the londe of galyce and of
galylee, by hys holy grace, and he whom herode dyd 28
put to deth by swerde; and my body abydeth emonge
the sarasyns, whyche haue entreated it vylaynsly, &

and reproaches
him for not
recovering that
country from the
Saracens,

lyeth in a place whyche is not knowen.   But I merueylle that thou hast not conquerd my londe, Seen and 32
consyderyd that thou hast conquerd so many regyones,
townes, & cytees in the world.   wherfore I do the to
wete, that lyke as god hath chosen the, and made the

¹ k v, back.

superyor in worldly puyssaunce aboue al other kynges
& worldly prynces, in lyke wyse emong al them that
lyuen thou art chosen of god, after the conduyte of
4 the sterres, to delyuer my londe fro the hande of the
mescreaunt sarasyns and enemyes of crystendom. ¶ And
to thende that thou sholdest knowe in to what ¹place
thou sholdest goo, thou hast seen on the heuen the
8 sterres by dyuyne magnyfycence.   And for to obteyne
the more Ioye & gretter glorye in heuen, by haultayn
and grete puyssaunce, thou shalt surmounte thyn enemyes, & in that same place thou sha[l]t make and doo
12 edefye a chyrche in my name, to the whiche shal come
the crysten peple of al regyons, for to gete helthe &
pardon of their synnes.   After that thou shalt haue
vysited my sepulture, and haue made the waye sure, and
16 ordeyned crysten men for to kepe and conserue the
place, it shal be a memoyre perpetuell."   Thus in thys
maner appyered thre tymes saynt Iames to the emperour
Charles.   After these vysyons and certyfycacyons of
20 god, he called and assembled hys subgettes, whome he
dyd do put a grete multytude in good poynte, & after
took hys waye & drewe toward the contre where the
sterres had shewed the waye aforesayd, and came fyrst
24 in to spayne : and the fyrst cyte that was rebelle to hym
was panpylonne, whyche was ryght stronge of murayl
and towres, & garnysshed wyth sarasyns.   and he
abode tofore it thre monethes, or he coude fynde maner
28 to confounde it.   Thenne Charles knewe not what to
do, but to praye god and saynt Iames, for whom he
went, ²that in the vertu of hys name he myght take
that cyte, and sayd in thys manere : "Fayr lord god,
32 my maker, helpe me that am comen in to thys contree
for to enhaunce the crysten fayth, for to establysshe
and mayntene thyn holy name.   And also thou holy
saynt Iames, by the reuelacyon of whome I am in thys

Marginal notes:
as God wishes him.

He promises him success, and bids him raise a church to his name,

as a perpetual memorial.

After this vision had appeared thrice,

Charles starts with his army for Galicia.

He besieges Pampeluna in vain for three months,

and then invokes in prayer the help of St. James.

¹ k v, back, col. 2.   ² k vj.

Iourneye, I requyre the that I may subdewe thys cytee,
& entre therin, for to shewe the mysbyleuyng[1] peple the
cause of theyr errour, to thende that this begynnyng
may the better determyne the ende of myn entencyon." 4

Immediately after
his prayer the
walls of the city
fall down.
Assone as Charles had[1] fynysshed[1] his oryson, the
walles of the cyte, whyche were of marble merueillously
strong, ouerthrew to the erthe, & fyl alle in pyeces;
and[1] after, charles and his hoost entred[1] in to the cyte ; 8
& he that wold[1] be baptysed[1] & byleue in god[1] wythoute
fyctyon, was saued[1] and put a-parte, and who sayd[1] the
contrarye, was forthwyth put to deth. Al the people of
that contre, whan they knewe of these tydynges & 12
meruayllous operacyons of this cyte, torned[1] in to Ruyne
at the symple postulacyon of charles, without contra-

All the country
yields to Charles,
who causes the
people to be bap-
tised, and builds
churches.
dyctyon came and[1] yelded[1] them to the mercy of kyng[1]
charles. And[1] thus many were baptysed[1], and chyrches 16
were ordeyned[1], and[1] al the contreye redu[1]ced to certeyn
trybute vnder the fydelyte of the emperour charles, and[1]
brought theyr trybutes fro the cytees wyth-oute ony
other gaynsayeng in sygne of seygnourye.   20

¶ Of the cytees goten in espayne by charles,
    & how somme were by hym destroyed'.
    [capitulo   ij.]

AFter that charles had[1] the domynacyon quasi in al 24
Charles arrives at
the tomb of St.
James,
espayne, he came to the sepulture of Saynt Iames,
where he dyd[1] hys deuocyon, and[1] made deuoutely hys
prayers ; & after came to a place in þe lond whych was
so ferre, that he myght goo no ferther, and[1] there fyxed[1] 28
& pyght hys spere, and that place was called[1] petro-
nium ; & thanked[1] god and saynt Iames, that by theyr
suffrau*n*ce he was comen so ferre wythoute ony contradyctyon surely vnto suche place that he myght passe 32
no ferther. And[1] in that londe who that wold[1] byleue

in god, tharchebysshop Turpyn baptysed them ; & who
that wold not, he was slayn, or put in pryson. And after
Charles wente from one see to that other, and thenne he
4 gate in galyce xiij cytees, emonge whome compostelle
was thenne the leste. In espayne he had xvj grete
townes & stronge, emonge whome ¹was onsea, in which
were wont to be x stronge toures, & a toun named
8 petrosse, in whyche was made the fynest syluer that
had thenne cours. Also another cyte named attentyua,
where as the body of saynt Torquete rested, whyche was
dyscyple of saynt Iames, and there vpon the sepulture
12 was an olyue tree, [whyche dyd] florysshe & bere rype
fruyt a certayn day of may euery yere withoute fayllyng.

Alle the contreye of spayne that tyme was subgette
to charles, That is to wete, the londe of alandaluf, the
16 londe of perdoures, the londe of castellans, the londe of
maures, The londe of portyngale, the londe of sarasyns,
the londe of nauarre, the londe of Alemans, The londe
of byscoys, the londe of bascles, the londe of palargyens,
20 and somme of theyr cytees taken by warre, subtyl and
mortal, And somme wythoute warre. he coude not
wynne the grete towne of Lucerne, tyl at the laste he
layed syege tofore it by the space of foure monethes.
24 and it stode in a grene valeye. And after, whan he saw
that they wold not yelde them, & that he coude not
wynne them, he made hys prayer vnto god, and to
saynt Iames, that he myght be vyctorious, seen that he
28 had nomore to termyne in that contreye, but that cyte
onely. hys oryson was herde, soo that ²the walles fyl
doun to the erthe, and was put to destructyon in suche
wyse, þat neuer man dwelled therin after, and after it
32 sanke, and therin was an abysme or swolowe of water,
In whyche were founden after, fysshes alle blacke.
Emonge the other cytees that he took, there were iiij
that dyd hym moche payne, or he myght gete them, &

¹ k vj, back.   ² k vj, back, col. 2,

He captures 13
cities in Galicia,
and 16 in Spain,

the whole of
which was subject
to him.

He besieges
Lucerne for 4
months,

but in vain,

and then prays to
St. James,

when the walls
fall down, and
the city is taken,

and turned into a
lake containing
black fishes.

therfore he gaf them the maladyctyon of god, and they
were cursed, in suche wyse that vnto thys day there is
in them none habytacion; & the sayd cytees been
named lucerne, ventose, caperee, & adame.   4

¶ Of the grete ydole that was in a cyte,
whyche coude not be smyton doun, and
of the condycyons and' sygnes therof:
ca.   iij 8

WHan Charles had doon in spayne & other places,
wyth the Inhabytauntes of it at hys wylle, Alle
thydolles and other symylacres that he fonde, he dyd
do destroye and put to confusyon. But in the londe of 12
Alandaluf, in a cyte called Salancadys, in arabyque, was[1]
the place of a grete god, as the sarasyns sayd. That
ydolle was made of the honde of Machommete in the
tyme that he lyued, & was named Mahommet [2]in 16
thonour of hym: and by arte magyke and dyabolyke
he closed therin a legyon of deuylles, for to kepe it and
make sygnes for to abuse the peple. and thys ydolle was
kepte so by deuylles, that noo persone lyuyng coude by 20
strengthe destroye it, ne put it doun. In suche wyse
that yf ony crysten man came nyghe for to see it, or to
coniure it, or to destroye, Assone as he began to coniure
and preche, anon he was perysshed & destroyed. And 24
the sarasyns that came for to preche, adoure, make
sacrefyse, or doo obeyssaunce therto, were wythout
peryl; and yf by aduenture, a byrde fleyng came &
rested vpon it, Incontynent it was deed. The stone 28
vpon whyche thydolle was sette was meruayllously
made. It was a stone of the see, wrought of sarasyns,
and grauen subtylly of grete and ryche facyon, the
whyche was enhaunced vpryght, not without grete 32
crafte & connyng. toward the erth it was meruayllously

Marginal notes:
Charles destroys all the idols;
but at Salancadys was a great idol,
kept so by devils that none could destroy it,
and which no Christian dare approach.
It stood on a large stone, richly carved,

[1] orig. and was.   [2] k vij.

grete, & alway vpward it was lasse ; and that stone was
so hye as a crowe myght flee : vpon whyche stone was
thydolle sette, whyche was of fyn yuorye, after thas- *and was of fine ivory,*
4 semblaunce of a man stondyng vpryght on his feet, &
had hys face torned to the south, & helde in his ryght *and held in his hand a key,*
honde a grete keye, & the sarasyns were certefyed ¹for
trouthe that whan a kyng of fraunce shold be borne,
8 & in strengthe to subdue the contreye of spayne, and
brynge it in to crysten fayth, the ymage shold lete falle *which was to fall when a king should come to subdue the country,*
the keye, whych shold be a sygne þat the kyng of
fraunce shold conquere them.   So thenne in the tyme
12 that the noble kyng charles regned in spayne, for to
brynge it to the crysten faith, the ydolle lete the keye *On the approach of Charles the key falls.*
falle doun to the grounde.   And whan the sarasyns
sawe that, They hydde theyr tresours, as golde, syluer,
16 and precyous stoones, in therth, by cause the crysten
men shold no thynge fynde therof, & they al wente in
to another regyon, and durst not abyde the comyng of
the kyng.

20 ¶ Of the chyrche of saynt Iames in galyce,
   and' of dyuers other whyche Kyng' Charles
   founded : capitulo   iiij

   CHarles beyng in galyce had Innumerable quantyte *Charles, having an immense quantity of gold and silver,*
24 of gold, of syluer, and of precyous stones, of many
   kynges, prynces, and other lordes, and of trybutes of
   cytees that was gyuen to hym as lord.
   ¶ Also he had moche of the tresour that he conquerd
28 of the townes and contreyes of Spayne ²aforesayd.
   Thenne he, seyng the grete habundaunce of good, dyd
   do compose and make a chirche of Saynt Iames, in the *builds a church to St. James,*
   place where-as he had founde the body of hym.   and
32 he abode there the space of thre yere wythout departyng,
   and in that same place he ordeyned a bysshop, and *and ordains a bishop*

¹ k vij, col. 2.   ² k vij, back.

and three canons.

founded there chanonnes reguler, vnder the rule of
saynt Ysodore the confessour; & bought & ordeyned

He endows the church,

for them rentes & trybutes suffycyent, and gaf to them
synguler seygnourye. He furnysshed the chyrche wyth 4

and supplies vestments and ornaments.

belles, vessellys of golde and syluer, adournements of
precyous clothes, & al thynges necessarye & apper-
teynyng in a chyrche pontyfycal. also of bokes, vesty-
mentes, chalyces, & other holy escryptures. And of 8
the resydue of gold and syluer, that he brought oute of
spayne, he dyd doo edefye these chyrches folowyng.

Another church he builds at Acon to Our Lady,

¶ Fyrst, at Acon, in almayne, where as he is buryed,
he dyd doo make a chirche of our lady; and though it 12
be lytel, yet is it moche rychely made. The chyrche

and four to St. James,

of Saynt Iames in the toun of vyterbe; also the chyrche
of saynt Iames in the cytee of Tholouse : The chyrche
of Saynt Iames in gascoyne; also the chirche of saynt 16
Iames in parys, bytwene the sayne & the mounte of
martres. & aboue the chyrches aforesayd, he founded,

besides abbeys and monasteries.

rented, & releued many & dyuers chyrches, monasteryes,
& other abbeyes in the world, in many and dyuers 20
places.

¶ How, after that Aygolant the geaunt had
taken spayne & put to deth the crysten
people, Charles recouerd' it, and' other 24
maters : capitulo   v

After Charles's return to France,

After that charles was retorned in to Fraunce, a

Algolant, an African giant, reconquers Spain,

kyng sarasyn of affryque, named aygolant, wyth
grete puyssaunce came in to spayne, and remysed it in 28
hys subgectyon. And the crysten which charles had

and puts the Christians to death.

left there, as many as he myght gete, he put to deth,
and the other fledde. And in shorte tyme the tydynges
came vnto kyng Charles, wherof he was moche abasshed 32
& angry, bycause it was shewed to hym so pyetously.

¹ k vij, back, col. 2.

wherfore Incontynent he assembled a grete hoost, &
wyth a grete multytude of fyghtyng men he went
thyder wythout taryeng. And he made the conduytour   Milo, Roland's
father, is put in
4 of them al Myllon of angleres, the fader of Rolland. &   command.
they cessed not tyl that they had tydynges where
Aygolant the geaunt was, whyche had doon thys feat.
whan charles knewe where Aygolant was lodged, [1] and
8 semblably aygolant knewe where Charles was, Anone
the geaunt sente to charles that he wold delyuer bataylle   Aigolant chal-
lenges any num-
suche as he wold. That is to wete that Charles shold   ber of Charles's
men to fight
sende to hym xx of hys men to fyght ageynst xx of hys   against an equal
number of his.
12 sarasyns, or xl ayenst xl, or an C ayenst C, or a thousand
ayenst a thousand, or two men ayenst two, or one man
ayenst one man onely. kyng Charles, seyng thenten-
cyon of aygolant, for thonour of noblesse he wold not
16 refuse hys demaunde, but sent to hym an C knyghtes   Charles sends 100
knights,
in grete poynte, and the geaunte sente another hondred
ayenst the crysten men, but anone the sarasyns were   who slay the 100
Saracens;
vanquysshed & put to deth, and after were sente by
20 aygolant two hondred sarasyns ayenst two hondred   and after 200,
who also kill their
crysten men, whyche Sarasyns were anone wythoute   opponents.
grete resystence put to deth and slayn. Aygolant was
not contente, ne wold not leue herby, but sente two   Aigolant sends
2000 Saracens,
24 thousand sarasyns ayenst ij M crysten men, and whan
they were in batayll, many of þe sarasyns were slayn,   but they also are
defeated.
and the other put to flyght for to saue them self. The
thyrd day after, Aygolant maad certeyn experyences,
28 and knewe. that yf Charles made warre to hym he
shold haue grete losse, and sent to Charles to wete yf
he wold make playne warre. Charles [2] was contente,
and there vpon they made redy theyr peple, and   Both sides prepare
for a general
32 specyally charles, for hys subgettes had grete affectyon   engagement.
to goo to bataylle without ony fere of deth. And also
somme of the crysten men, the day tofore the bataylle,
dyd do amende and araye theyr harnoys, and sette

¹ k viij.   ² k viij, col. 2.

theyr tentes nygh a ryuer named ceye, and pyght there
theyr speres, euen in the place where as the bodyes of
saynt faconde and saynt premytyf rested, where after
was made a chyrche deuoutely founded, and also a 4
stronge cyte by the moyen of the sayd Charles, and in
the place where the speres were pyght, our lord shewed

grete myracle.   For of them that shold deye there and
be gloryfyed marters of god & crowned in heuen, theyr 8
speres on þᵉ morn were founden al grene, floresshed
and leued, whyche was a precedent sygne that they
whyche shold deye shold haue the Ioye in heuen.

¶ Eche man took his owne, and cutte of the bowes & 12
leues, wyth whyche the leues were planted and vnder-
roted, wherof in a lytel whyle after grewe a grete wode,
whyche stondeth there yet.   It was grete meruayle of
the Ioye that the horses made, whyche dyd theyr 16
deuoyrs as wel as the men after theyr qualyte, whyche
was a grete token.   Thenne L valyaunt [1]crysten men
were slayne, And emonge the other was slayne duc
Myllon, fader to Roulland.   Also that same day the 20
hors of charles was slayn vnder hym, & whan he was a
fote he maad grete murdre wyth hys swerde Ioyouse,
and dyd so moche that the sarasyns, dredyng the
euenyng, fledde & wythdrewe them in to place of 24
surete.   And as it was the wylle of our lord, the next
day after came to Charles in to his helpe iiij marquyse
of ytalye, accompanyed wyth iiij M stronge fyghtyng
men & chosen.   wherfore Aygolant, assone as he knewe 28
of theyr comyng, he fled and wythdrewe hym ouer the
see toward hys contree. but they myȝt not for hast bere
with them al theyr tresours, wherfor fraunce was
enryched meruayllously aboue alle other contrees.   32
¶ And whan charles sawe his departyng he came
wyth al hys rychesse in to fraunce, and thenne, duryng
seuen yere, he dyd do ordeyne the seruyce and offyce of

[1] k viij, back.

the chyrche by preestes & clerkes, and the festes of
sayntes of all the yere ; and grete vertu & meruayllous
effect was compryse̔d in thys man.   For whan it was
4 not warre for to mynysshe thynfydellys and encreace the
crysten fayth, For tenhaunce the name of god he made
the offyces and legendes of holy sayntes, & dyd [1]reduce
in to mynde and remembraunce the passyons of holy
8 marters in establysshyng theyr feestes, to thende that
we sholḍ ensyewe them, and to eschewe al cuyl.   And
the magnytude of thys kyng was wel preue̔d by sygnes
seen on the heuen.   For in the same yere the mone
12 derke̔d thre tymes, and the sonne ones, and companyes
of people were seen meruayllous, whyche shewe̔d that
thys Charles was of grete magnytude, that is to wete
bytwene heuen and erthe.

and occupies himself in drawing up rules and services for the Church.

This year were three eclipses of the moon, and one of the sun.

16 ¶ How Aygolant sent to charles that he shold'
     come to hym trustely for to make Iust
     warre, and' how Charles in habyte dys-
     symyled' spake to hym, and' of other
20   maters : capitulo   vj

A S I haue sayd the kyn[ge,] Aygolant the geaunte,
     fledde in to hys contreye, whan socours cam to
     Charles of foure marques. he slepte not vpon his
24 purpoos, but maad grete dylygence for to assemble hys
people, whyche were sarasyns Innumerable, for he
assemble̔d mores, Moabytes, Ethiopiens, Affrycans, and
percyens ; he brought wyth hym also the kyng of
28 arabye, the kyng of barbarye, the kyng of malroste, the
kyng of [2]maioryke, the kyng of meques, the kyng of
cybylle, & the kyng of Cordube, the whych cam with
peple wythout nombre, certain, in to gascoyne, in to a
32 stronge cyte named Agenne, and took it.   And after
sent to Charles that he sholḍ come to hym peasybly &

Aigolant collects an immense army,

and again invades Gascony, and captures the city of Agenne.

----

[1] k viij, back, col. 2.   [2] l j.

Aigolant invites
Charles to visit
him unattended.

trustyly, with a fewe peple, promysyng¹ to hym for to
gyue to hym ix hors laden with gold, syluer, and¹ precyous stones, yf he wold¹ thus come at hys desyre. this
paynym shewed to hym this by cause he wold knowe 4
his persone, for hys strengthe & puyssaunce knewe he
wel by experyence, and¹ also to thende whan he knewe
hym that he myght in the warre flee hym. whan kyng¹
charles knewe this mandement he gadred not grete 8

Charles sets out
with 2000 knights,

peple, but he came onely wyth ij M knyghtes of honour
and of grete strength. And¹ whan he was foure myle
nygh the cyte, where Aygolant and al the kynges tofore

whom he leaves,
except 40,
near the city.

named were, he left his people secretly, & came vnto a 12
mountayne nygh the cyte, accompanyed¹ wyth xl
knyghtes onely. And fro thys place they saw the cyte,
by cause to wete yf the multytude of peple were de-
parted¹, soo that he shold¹ not be deceyued¹. Neuertheles 16
vpon thys montayne he lefte hys people secretly, and

He himself, in
disguise and with
only one attend-
ant, enters the
city,

took of hys clothes, and cladde hym in the guyse of a
messager, and¹ ¹took one knyght onely with hym,
whyche bare his spere & swerde and¹ bocler vnder hys 20
mantel, and¹ soo came in to the cyte, and anone he was
brought tofore aygolaunt the geaunt. And whan he was

and presents him-
self as a messenger
from Charles,

tofore hym he sayd¹ in thys manere : " Charles the kyng
hath sente vs vnto the, and¹ leteth the wete by vs that 24

to say he had
come with only
40 attendants.

he is comen lyke as thou hast comanded¹, accompanyed¹
wyth fourty knyghtes onely, for to do that he ought to
doo. Now thenne come to hym wyth xl knyghtes,
withoute moo, yf thou wylt accomplysshe and holde 28
that thou hast promysed¹." Aygolant sayd¹ to hem that
they shold¹ retorne to charles, and¹ that they shold say

Aigolant replies
that he will go
and meet the
French king.

to hym that he departe not, but abyde hym there, and¹
he wold¹ come and¹ vysyte hym. After this that charles 32
had¹ knowen the geaunt, and after vysyted¹ the towne,
for to knowe the feblest parte for to take and conquer
it whan he shold come ageyn, & sawe al the kynges

¹ l j, col. 2.

forsayd & their puyssaunces, he after retorned to his
peple whiche he had left vpon the montayne, & after
came to hys ij M knyghtes.   & anone after aygolant,
4 accompanyed wyth vij M kny3tes, came after them
withoute taryeng.   But charles took hede whan he cam
that there were many moo paynyms than crysten men,
and ¹wythout lenger taryeng charles & his peple de-
8 parted, and retourned in to fraunce wythout hauyng
other delyberacyon.

Charles, having spied out all the city, departs.

Aigolant, with 7000 men, follows him,

but Charles escapes.

¶ How Charles, accompanyed with moche
peple, retorned' in to the place aforesayd &
12   toke the cyte of agenne, & other maters :
[capitulo]   vij

Fter that cnarles was retorned in to fraunce he
assembled moche peple, & after came to the cyte
16   of agenne, & assyeged it there by grete facyon,
the space of vij monethes.   Aygolant was therin &
many sarasyns, & the crysten men had made fortressis
& castelles of tree tofore this cyte for to greue it.   Whan
20 Aygolant & the grete lordes of his companye sawe þat
they myght not endure, they maad hooles & caues vnder
therth for tescape oute secretly : in that maner they came
out of the cyte, & passed ouer a ryuer, which ranne by
24 the cyte, named goronna, and so they saued them self.
The next day after, whan there was noo grete resystence made to the crysten men, Charles wyth grete
tryumphe & puyssaunce entred in to the cyte, & put to
28 deth x M sarasyns that he there fonde.   The other,
seyng that, put them to flyght by the ryuer.   Aygolant
²was in another stronge toun, & whan charles knewe it
he came thyder & assaylled it, & sente to hym to delyuer
32 ouer the cyte.   aygolant ansuerd that he wold not so
doo, but by a moyen that was, that they shold make a

Charles assembles a large army,

and lays siege to Agenne, which he surrounds.

Aigolant and his lords escape by mines.

Charles enters the city,

and after besieges the city to which Aigolant had fled.

¹ l j, back.   ² l j, back, col. 2.

Aigolant proposes a general battle.

batayll, & he that shold wynne the bataylle shold be
lorde of þe toun, & so they assygned the day of the
bataylle. and nygh to that place, bytwene the castel
thalabourt & a ryuer called carantha, somme of the 4
crysten men planted theyr speres in the grounde, especially they that on the morn shold deye, & obteyne the

Those of the Christians who were destined to die are again pointed out by a miracle.

crowne of glorye as marters of god. and on the morne
they fonde their speres al grene & myraculously leued, 8
& ful of bowes, wherof the cristen men were moche
Ioyous of this myracle, and raught not for to deye for
þe crysten fayth in mayntenyng the name of god.
After that they cutte of theyr speres and wente to 12

The Saracens are utterly defeated.

bataylle, and put many sarasyns to deth. But in
thende were slayn and martred, of crysten men moo
than iiij M whyche were saued in heuen ; & that tyme
the hors that Charles rode on was slayn vnder hym, 16
and at that bataylle were slayn by the sayd Charles the
kynge of Agabyc [&] the kyng of bugye, merueyllous
myghty sarasyns.

[1]¶ Of the vertuous operacions that charles 20
made whan he was retorned' in to fraunce,
& what barons he had' in hys companye, &
of theyr puyssaunce : ca.   viij

After his defeat Aigolant flies to Pampeluna.

THe bataylle toforesayd made, Aygolant fledde and 24
came in to panpylone, and sent to kyng charles
that he shold abyde hym for to gyue hym bataylle
more ample & large. Whan charles knewe hys desyre

Charles returns to France for reinforcements.

he retourned in to fraunce for to haue helpe of hys 28
peple, and made an open maundement thorugh out al
Fraunce that al maner peple that were of euyl condycyon
and in bondage, that they that were present, and theyr
successours, shold be free, & there vpon tabellyons shold 32
be delyuerd accordyng to the lawe, that wold goo with

[1] l ij.

hym ayenst the myscreauntes.   Also alle prysonners
that were in fraunce, he delyuerd them al out of   He frees all prisoners,
pryson, & to al them that shold haue ben delyuerd to
4 deth for felonnye, murdre, or treason, he pardonned
them & gaf to them theyr lyf; and to al poure peple
that had not wherby to lyue, he gaf to them good
largely, & them that were euyll clad, he clothed them   clothes the poor,
8 after theyr degree.   alle them that were at debate he
peased them & accorded; Alle them þat were dys-
heryted & put oute from theyr lyuelode he restored al   restores the disinherited,
to them; Alle þe peple¹ that myght bere armes he
12 armed them.   The valyaunt squyers of theyr persones   and raises the esquires to
he made knyghtes, & al them that were in hys Indyg-   knighthood, on condition of
nacyon & pryued [f]ro hys loue, & bannysshed for the   joining his army.
loue of god, he was constraynede to pardonne them, &
16 made pees with euery man.   and thenne he was four-
nysshed of moo than an C thousand men wel fyghtyng,
wythoute them that were a-fote, whyche were Innumerable.   And for to gyue courage to the prynces of Charles,
20 Turpyn sayd in this maner: "I, Turpyn, archebysshop   Turpin assures him of success.
of Raynes by the grace of god, shal gyue good courage
to crysten people, and shal slee the Infydels, sarasyns,
with myn owne handes."   ¶ Wyth Charles was   With Charles are Roland, Oliver,
24 Roulland of Cenonye, neuewe of Charles, sone of hys   and Aristagius with 14,000 men.
syster, dame Berthe, & of Duke Myllon, wyth foure
thousand fyghtyng men; Olyuer, duc of genes, sone of
duc Reyner, with iij M fyghtyng men: Aristagius,
28 kyng of brytayne, wyth vij thousand fyghtyng men;
Not wythstondyng that in brytayne was another kyng,
Eugelius, whyche was duke of Guyan, whome Au-   Besides were men from Guienne,
gustus Cezar had ordeyned, wyth the byturyciens, tho
32 monyques, pictauyns, scauctonens, and Elogysmes,
cytees with their prouynces vnder guyan: & he cam
with iij M horsmen ²good fyghtars; Garferus, kyng
of bordeloys, with iiij M men; Salamon, felow of estok;

¹ l ij, col. 2.   ² l ij, back.

bawdewyn, brother of Rolland; Naymes, duc of bauyere,
wyth x M fyghtyng' men; Hoel of Nauntes, &

Burgundy,
Lambert, prynce of bourgoyn, wyth ij M fyghtars;
Sanson, duc of bourgoyn, with x M; Garyn, duc of 4

Lorraine, and
other provinces.
lorayne, & many other; and Charles had of his
owne contre moo than fyfty M men. The excercyte
of Charles, the noble emperour, and ryght puyssaunt
kyng' of Fraunce, was so grete and so ample that it helde 8
two iourneyes longe, & in brede half o iourneye &
more; In suche wyse that of the bruyt that was made
for the grete multytude of the frensshemen, it was herde
two myle ferre and more.   12

¶ Of the tryews of Charles & of Aygolant,
and of the deth of hys peple, & wherfore
aygolant was not baptysed': capitulo   ix

THe whyl that charles was a yonge chylde he 16
lerned at Toulete the langage of sarasyns, and

Aigolant, fright-
ened at the num-
bers of the French,
spake it whan he wold. Aygolant, thys geaunt
and grete Lord, coude not absteyne hym, and cam
nygh vnto crystyente, and sente to Charles to come to 20

proposes a con-
ference.
hym vnto Pampylone, and tryews was [1]maad bytwene
them. For Aygolant consyderyd the multytude of hys
people and the puyssaunces of their persones. For by
cours of nature hym semed he shold surmounte the 24
crysten peple, but he thought that the god of crysten
people was more certayn and trewe than the god of the
paynyms; but er he wold declyne fro the worshyppyng of
hys goddes, he had desyre to assaye yet ones the nombre 28
of paynyms ayenst the nombre of crysten men. And

It is agreed to
leave the question
of religion to a
trial of arms
between equal
numbers.
he was contente to make a pacte and couenaunt wyth
charles, that he that shold obteyne the vyctorye vpon
others peple, that his god were holden and worshypped, 32
And that the god of hym that shold lose the bataylle

[1] l ij, back, col. 2.

sholď be of noo valure, renyeď, anď reputeď for nought.
Anď vpon thys couenaunte were sente twenty crysten
knyghtes ayenst xx knyghtes paynyms.   Anď anone
4 as they were assembleď anď medleď to-gyder, the twenty
sarasyns were slayn. Anď after were sente fourty ayenst
fourty, Anď anone the sarasyns were slayn anď vayn-
quyssheď.   Anď after he sent an C. ayenst an C., but
8 they were not slayne, but fledde. Aygolant thouȝt he
wold do better, anď sent ij hondred ayenst ij C., anď
anone the sarasyns were ouercomen & slayn. ¹¶ Thys
geaunt was euyl contente of the destructyon of hys
12 peple, and for to make a grete descomfyte, he sente a
thousanď sarasyns ayenst a M cristen men, anď wythoute makyngᵗ grete rebellyon, the sarasyns were anone
slayn anď put to deth. Thenne the kyngᵗ Aygolant, by
16 experyence for-made, afermed the fayth & the lawe of
crysten peple to be better, more sure, & more certeyn
than the lawe of the paynyms and sarasyns, and thus he
was enclyneď to the crysten fayth, & dysposeď hym to
20 receyue baptym on the morne without fayntyse ; and
here vpon he demandeď tryews anď surete for to goo &
come to Charles, & he graunteď it to hym wyth gooď
hert.   anď thus atte houre of tyerce, whan charles was
24 at dyner, Aygolant haď entencyon to see charles ˋand
hys maner at mete, for to knowe hys astate, yf it were
vayllerous anď soo grete as it was in armes and in
batáylles.   And also he came pryncypally for to be
28 baptyseď, anď he sawe Charles at hys table with grete
magnyfycence, and after beholde the ordre of hys peple
and sawe that somme were in habyte of knyghtes and
grete prynces, Other in habyte of chanons & monkes ;
32 & asked so that he was certefyed of euery ordre, anď
the cause of theyr estate, and after ²that he sawe
in a parte of yᵉ halle syttyng on the grounde, xiij
poure persones, which dyned & ete as other dyď.   for

20 Christians
engage as many
Saracens, and
slay them;

and after 40 over-
come 40 Saracens;

and finally 1000
Christians slay
1000 Saracens.

Aigolant is con-
vinced, and agrees
to receive baptism.

He asks to see
Charles at meat
with his lords.

He sees 13 poor
men, sitting on
the ground at
dinner,

¹ l iij.   ² l iij, col. 2.

charles of custom wold not take his repaste tyl he
had xiij poure men in the worsͪypp of our lord and
of his xij appostles, & he toke hede how these poure
men satte on the grounde without towayl in ryght poure 4

habyte, & dyned al soroufully, & he demaundeꝺ what
people they were.   Charles ansuerꝺ & sayꝺ : " they be
goddes peple anꝺ messagers of our lorꝺ Ihesu cryst,
whome I susteyne in thonour of hym & his xij appostles 8
that he haꝺ with hym, & gyue to them refectyon cor-
porel." Aygolant said : " certeynlye he serueth euyl
hys lord yᵗ receyueth his messagers in thys manere. I
see wel that they that ben aboute the been in good 12
poynt & wel arayed, & wel serued of mete & drynke,
& the seruauntes of thy god lyue pourely & euyl clothed
ayenst yᵉ colde, & ben withdrawen ferre fro the. he
dooth grete shame to his lorꝺ that receyueth his mes- 16
sagers in this manere. & more ouer, I see now wel that
the lawe whyche thou hast sayd to me to be gooꝺ &
holy, by thy werkes thou sͪewest them to be fals & of
no valewe." & herof aygolant was all mocued & troubled 20
in his entendement, & he beyng put out alle fro hys
purpose, toke leue of the ¹kyngꞏ & retourneꝺ to hys
peple, & renounceꝺ to be baptyseꝺ, and sente worꝺ to
charles for to begynne warre ageyn on yᵉ morne more 24
stronge than euer he haꝺ doon tofore.

¶ Of the deth of aygolant and of his peple, &
   how moche crysten peple were slayn by
   concupyscence of syluer, & of crysten men 28
   founden dede by myracle : [ca.]   x

W Han charles sawe Aygolant come for to baptyse
hym he was moche Ioyous, but whan he re-
torneꝺ & forsoke it he was euyl contente, & 32
took aduys vpon the pour men whyche he sayꝺ were

¹ l iij, back.

messagers of god. For after the pouerte of them, and
after that they were named, fore to holde them so, was
none honour to theyr mayster, & the emperour re-
4 membred wel that the peple of god ought to be receyued honestly, & honourably holden & serued. wherfor
the poure men that he fonde in thexcercyte he dyd
them to be wel clothed & honestly, and gaf to them
8 mete largely, And took suche custome in hym self that
he faylled not, but the pour peple were receyued with
honour in his companye. vpon thys purpose on a day
folowyng, the sarasyns put them to bataylle, and to
12 fyght [1]ayenst the crysten men by grete fyerste, and
there was soo grete destructyon that day of the sarasyns,
that the crysten men were empesshed and lette by the
blood that ranne so habundantly, as it had rayned many
16 dayes water and blood. wherefore [2] Aygolant, seyng
the destructyon of his people as he that doubted nothyng
to deye, aduaunced [3] so hym self that he was slayn and
put to deth, and after the cristen men entred in to the
20 cyte of pampylone, and put to deth al the sarasyns that
they fonde therin.

Thenne the kyng of Cybylle & the kyng of cordube
saued them self with somme of their subgettes. After
24 thys the crysten men ful of couetyse for to haue gold
and syluer of the sarasyns that were deed retorned, And
whan they were wel charged & laden wyth golde, syluer,
and other hauoyr, the kyng of Cybylle and the kyng
28 of Cordube took hede ther of, And wyth al their meyne
came couertly vpon the crysten men, and put to deth
moo than a thousand.

¶ Thus may be knowen that the ardeur of concupy-
32 scence was cause of the deth of the soule wythoute
vyctorye, and to god dysplaysaunte. ¶ On the morne
tydynges came how so many sarasyns were slayn, and

and has all these poor men clothed and honourably treated.

A great battle takes place,

in which the Saracens are defeated,

and Aigolant himself slain.

The kings of Seville and of Cordova fall on the Christians laden with booty, and kill more than 1000,

from which we may see the danger of covetousness.

[1] l iij, back, col. 2.   [2] *orig.* wherforr.
[3] *orig.* and aduaunced.

The king of Navarro chal-lenges Charles.

He accepts, and prays to God to point out which of the Christians are destined to die.

This being shown to him,

he locks them up in his chapel,

and goes to battle without them.

On his return he finds them all dead.

specyally of aygolant, vnto the prynce [1]of Nauarro
named Furre, wherfore he sent to Charles to haue
batayll ordynayre. Charles was so noble, so puyssaunt,
& so trustyng' in god', whan he faught for the crysten 4
fayth that he refused' hym not. and after, at the day of
batayle, whyche was assygned' on bothe partyes, Charles
put hym self to prayer, and' prayed' god deuoutely that
it plesed' hym, to shew what crysten men shold' deye in 8
that batayle. and on the day folowyng whan euery
man was armed' for to fyght, by the wylle of our lord
Charles sawe that same day the sygne of the crosse alle
redo vpon the sholdres behynde vpon theyr harnoys. 12
whan charles sawe it he thanked' our lord & had' com-
passyon of theyr deth, by cause of the valyaunce of
theyr persones. Thenne he sent for all them that bare
thensigne & made them to goo in to hys oratorye, and 16
after shette them fast therin, to the ende that they shold
not take deth that day ; and' thenne wyth al his other
hoost he went ayenst thoost of the prynce furre, but it
was not longe but furre and' hys people were destroyed' 20
and put to deth. and whan that was doon the emperour
came in to hys oratorye vyctoryous vpon hys enemyes,
and fonde al them that were shette wythin dede &
expyred', & thenne knewe[2] he wel that alle they that 24
were marked with the crosse were assygned that day to
be receyued in to heuen with glorye & crowne of marterdom, & that it apperteyned not to Charles to prolonge
theyr helthe. wherfore he is wel symple that wyl put 28
hym in payne to eschewe the passage of whyche he is
not maystre.

¶ Of feragus the merueyllous geaunt, how he
bare alwaye wyth hym the barons of fraunce 32
wyth out daunger, & how Roulland' faught
wyth hym: capitulo   xj.

[1] l iiij.   [2] l iiij, col. 2.

Fter that aygolant was slayn, & Furre, & many
kynges sarasyns as tofore is wryton, tho tydynges
cam to the admyral of babyloune, the which had a *The Amir of Babylon sends Ferragus, a marvellous giant,*
4 geant moche terryble, that was of the generacion of
golias, & he made hym to be accompanyed with xx M
turkes moche strong, and sente hym for to fyght ayenst
charles themperour. For hys puyssaunce was redoubted
8 thurgh tho world, & tho sayd feragus cam vnto the cyte
of vagyere, nygh to saynt Iames, bytwene cristendom
& hethenes, & sent to Charles that he shold come to *to fight against Charles.*
fyght ayenst hym. This geant was moche meruayllous,
12 For he doubted neyther spere ne swerde, ne arowe, ne
other shotte. And he had the strengthe of xl ¹myghty
men and stronge. Anone as Charles knewe the tydynges
of hys comyng, he went to hym and was vpon his
16 watche nygh by vagyere. Whan thys was knowen this
geaunte yssued oute of the towne, and demaunded syn- *He challenges any French knight.*
guler persone ayenst a persone. Charles, whiche neuer
had refused that to persone, sente to hym Ogyer the *Charles sends Ogier to meet him,*
20 danoys. but whan the geant sawe hym allone on the
felde, without makyng of ony semblaunte of warre, he
came allone to hym, & took hym wyth one hande & *but Ferragus takes him under*
put hym vnder hys arme, wythoute doynge to hym ony *his arm and*
24 harme, and bare hym vnto hys lodgys, and dyd do put
hym in pryson, and made nomore a-doo to bere hym, *carries him off,*
than dooth a wulf to bere a lytel lambe. The heyght *as a wolf would a lamb.*
of thys geaunt was of twelue cubytes : he had the face
28 a cubyte brode, the nose a palme longe, the armes &
thyes four cubytes long. The backe of his hand was
thre palmes longe. After that Ogyer was borne thus
awaye, Charles sente raynold daulbepyn. whan Feragus *Charles then sends Raynold,*
32 sawe hym, he bare hym a-waye as lyghtly as the other. *and he also is carried off.*
Charles was abasshed and sent tweyne other, that is to
wete, constayn of Rome, & therle hoel. This geaunt *Then Constayn and Hoel are sent,*
took that one wyth ² the ryght honde and that other

¹ l iiij, back.   ² *orig.* wyght.

but Ferragus carries them off, one in each hand.in the lyft honde, and bare them [1]bothe tweyne in-to pryson in to hys lodgyng, that euery man myght see. yet after charles sent other tweyne, and semblably they were bothe borne away wythoute ony wythstandyng or 4 contradyctyon. whan Charles saw the feet of this man, he was al abasshed, & durst nomore sende ony persone. For no man myght resyste hym.   Roulland, whyche was prynce of al thexcersyte of Charles, was euyl con- 8

Roland asks leave to fight the giant.

tente of thys that the geaunt was vyctoryous, & came to Charles and presented hym self for to goo fyght wyth hym, but charles wold not graunte hym.   At the last,

Charles reluctantly gives his consent.

by force, he was constrayned to gyue to hym lycence, 12 & Roulland made hym redy, and cam tofore Feragus;

Ferragus lifts Roland up with one hand, and lays him on his horse before him.

but anone he was taken and reteyned wyth hys ryght hande lyke the other, and the geaunt layed hym tofore hym on hys hors.   whan Rolland sawe that he was 16 taken & borne awaye soo vylaynsly he took a grete[2] courage in hym self, and called the name of Ihesus to

Roland, by an effort, overthrows the giant.

help, & to be in hys ayde, and torned hym ayenst Feragus, and took hym by the chynne, and made to 20 ouerthrowe fro hys hors, & fyl to the grounde, and rolland also.   And after anone they arose, and eueryche took hys owne hors.   Roulland, whyche was moche habyle and courageous, drewe [3]hys swerde durandal 24 and came ayenst the geaunt, and gaf soo grete a stroke

Roland kills the Saracen's horse,

on the Paynyms hors that he carf hym a-sondre in the myddes, and the paynym fyl to the erthe.   Feragus, beyng euyl contente for hys hors that was dede, took 28 hys swerde for to smyte Rolland, & had slayne hym wyth the stroke yf he had attayned hym; but assone as he lyfte vp hys arme for to haue smyton Rolland,

and wounds Ferragus in the arm.

Roulland auaunced hym self and smote the geant vpon 32 the arme, with whiche he helde hys swerde, suche a stroke, that hys swerde fyl to the grounde; wherof Feragus had grete despyte and supposed to haue smyten

[1] l iiij, back, col. 2.   [2] *orig.* gtete.   [3] l v.

hym wyth hys fyste, but he attayned rollandes hors in Roland's horse is killed.
suche wyse that he slewe hym. Thus were they bothe
two on fote, whyche wythoute swerd begynnen to fyght
4 wyth theyr fystes and wyth stones contynuelly, tyl the
houre of none : wherfore they bothe were wery, and Being both weary, they leave off fighting for the day.
took tryews to-gyder by one acorde vnto the morne,
and that they sholḍ fyght wythout spere and wythoute
8 hors : and here vpon eche of them went vn-to hys
lodgys.

¶ How on the morne rolland' and' Feragus
foughten & dysputeden the fayth, and by
12 what ¹moyen Feragus was slayn by Roulland' : capitulo   xij

THe next day folowyng⸗ erly, Rolland and Feragus Next morning the duel is renewed.
came to the felde of the bataylle. The geaunt
16 brought hys swerde moche grete, but it was nothynge
worth, for rollanḍ made prouysyon of a grete staffe or Roland takes with him only a great staff.
clubbe, ryȝt longe wyth whyche he smote the geaunt ;
but he myght nowher hurte hym. & also he smote
20 hym with grete stones and rounde, & coude in noo
wyse hurte ne entre in-to hys flesshe. And in this
maner they cessyd not to fyght tyl the houre of myd-
day. The geaunt was wery, and demaundeḍ tryews of At noon Ferragus is tired, and wishes to sleep a while.
24 Rollanḍ for to slepe and reste hym a lytel. Rolland
was contente, and was so noble and so valyaunt, that
whan the geaunt was layeḍ he went and fette a grete Roland makes him comfortable.
stone and layed it vnder hys heeḍ, to the ende that he
28 myght the better slepe and reste at hys ease. And
after that he haḍ a lytel slepte, & that he was awakeḍ,
he satte vp. And the noble Rollanḍ came and sat by
hym and sayḍ to hym : "I meruaylle moche of thy
32 feat, How thou art so stronge and so terryble that thou He asks him how it is he cannot by any means wound him.
mayst not be hurt ne wounꝺed in thy body by swerd,

¹ l v, col. 2.

Ferragus tells him that he is vulnerable only in the navel.

ne by staffe, ne by stones, ne in[1] [2]noo wyse." The
geaunt, which spake spaynyssh, saydᵉ to hym : "I may
not be slayn, but by the nauell." whan Rollandᵉ herde
that he made semblaunte that he vnderstoodᵉ hym not. 4
After Feragus demaunded hym what was hys name,
andᵉ of what lygnage he was. Rollandᵉ saydᵉ to hym :
"I am namedᵉ Rollandᵉ, and am neuew of charles, the
ryght myghty Emperour." & Feragus askedᵉ of hym 8
what lawe he helde.   Rollandᵉ ansuered : "I holde the
cristen fayth by the grace of god."   Feragus sayd :

The Saracen inquires about the doctrines of Christianity.

"what fayth is that, andᵉ who hath gyuen it?" to
whyche Roullandᵉ ansuerdᵉ : "It is trouthe yᵗ after god 12
almyȝty hadᵉ made heuen andᵉ erthe, andᵉ our fyrst fader
adam, which was dysobeyssaunt to hys commaundements ; the world was Jugod here in erthe wythoute

Roland tells him,

hauyngᵗ of beatytude, ne of felycyte : and long tyme 16
after the sone of god, the secondᵉ persone of the Trynyte,
remembredᵉ hym of the valure of the soule, the whiche
is gyuen to euery persone, andᵉ descendedᵉ fro heuen andᵉ
took our humanyte andᵉ suffredᵉ greuous passyon of 20
paynes.   Andᵉ he beyngᵗ in thys worldᵉ- hath gyuen en-
seygnements andᵉ stablyssedᵉ constytucyons for to saue

and how that all that are baptised shall be saved.

vs, & pryncypally who byleueth in hym & in hys
werkes parfyghtly, and that he be baptysedᵉ, After thys 24
[3]mortel lyf he shal be sauedᵉ in heuen : and, loo! thys
is the fayth that I holde, in the which I wyl deye."
Andᵉ after that Feragus hadᵉ made to hym many ques-
tyons in the fayth, and that Rollandᵉ hadᵉ ansuerdᵉ to 28
hym honourably in euery poynte, Feragus said in this
manere : "thou art crysten, andᵉ wylt maynteno the
fayth of whyche thou hast spoken, andᵉ I am a paynym,

Ferragus proposes to settle the question of religion by arms.

& holde for my god Mahoun.   who of vs tweyne that 32
shal be vanquysshedᵉ & ouercome, late hys lawe be
holde for nought andᵉ of noo valewe, and the fayth of
hym that is vyctoryous late it be holden for good &

¹ *orig.* im.   ² l v, back.   ³ l v, back, col. 2.

trewe, and that it be entyerly kepte and obserued."
The valyaunt Rolland was contente ryght wel, & ac- Roland agrees.
cepted hys langage.   thenne eche of them was redy to
4 fyght.   Anone Rolland came to hym, and Feragus lyft The fight is
vp hys arme for to smyte Rolland moche malycyously, renewed.
and Roulland sawe the stroke come vpon hym, and
for to voyde it he launced hys staffe ayenst the swerde,
8 and wyth the stroke the staffe was cutte asondre; and Roland's staff is
there-wythal the geaunt ranne to Rolland and had hym cut in two,
doun vnder hym.   Rolland, consyderyng that he myght
not flee ne escape, he called in hys hert deuoutely the
12 name of Ihesus, and yelded hym to god & ¹to the
vyrgyn marye : & he anon reprysed suche strengthe & but by a great
my3t that he aroos a lytel, & myghtyly repugned tho giant under him
geaunte, in suche manere that he brought the geaunte
16 vnder hym, and thenne moche quyckly and subtylly he
sete hande on hys swerde, and pryched hym in the and stabs him in
nauyll therwyth, & anone after aroos, and fledde al that the navel.
he my3t to thoost of charles.   Anone as feragus felte
20 hym self hurt in that place, he cryed so hye & lowde,
that alle they that were in that place were aferd &
abasshed of hys crye, & he sayd : "O Mahommet, my
god, to whom I haue gyuen my fayth, come & socour
24 me, for thou seest wel that I dye, and tarye noo lenger."
with that hydous voys the sarasyns camen to hym and The Saracens bear
bare hym awaye in theyr armes the best wyse they Ferragus away.
coude vnto hys lodgys ; and by that tyme rolland was
28 comen alle hool and sauf vnto Charles.   And forthwyth Charles assaults
the crysten men went Impetuously vpon the Sarasyns the town,
that bare Feragus, and entred in to the cyte, and so takes it and
moche dyd that the geaunt was dede, and after came
32 in to the pryson valyauntly, and took out Ogyer, releases his
Regnault, Constantyn, Hoel, and the other prysonners. knights.

¹ l vi.

¶ How Charles went to Cor-[1]dube, where the
kyng of the same place and' the kyng'
of Cybylle abode, for their destructyon :
ca.   xiij 4

The kings of
Cordova and
Seville defy
Charles,

AFter thys aforesayd, the kyng[1] Corbude and the
kyng[1] of Cybylle sent to Charles that he shold
come to cordube for to fyght.   Anone as charles knewe

who marches
against them.

it, he came thyder wyth all hys puyssaunce.   And 8
whan they were nygh for tassemble in bat", the
sarasyns maad a moche subtyl and wylde thynge.   For
tofore the Sarasyns that were on horsback they had
ordeyned men on fote, whyche had vysieres counter- 12
feyted all black & rede, horned, and berded lyke
deuylles, for to deceyue the crysten men ; and eueryche

The Saracens, by
a stratagem,

of these foot men bare in hys honde a lytel belle.   And
at thentre of the batylle they began to sowne and 16
make suche a bruyt, that assone as the horses of the
crysten men sawe them so counterfayted and sowne

frighten the
horses of the
Frenchmen,
and put them to
flight.

their bellys, so Impetuously they began to flee, disrenge
& to be aferde, in suche maner that no man might holde 20
theyr horses, but by force they must flee and wythdrawe

Charles devises a
remedy,

them.   Charles deuysed a remedye, and on the morne
he blynfelde the horses and couerd theyr eyen wyth
clothes, And stopped theyr eres, to the ende that they 24
shold not see ne [2]here the sarasyns dysguysed & coun-

and the battle is
renewed next
day.

trefayted.   And whan they came to batylle in this
manere they spared not, but slewe doun ryght, & put
the sarasyns to deth tyl mydday ; but yet they were 28
not al vaynquysshed, For they had a carte myghty and
grete for to resyste and make grete empesshement to
theyr enemyes.   And this engyne was drawen wyth

Of the standard
of the Saracens.

viij oxen in the warre, & ther-vpon[3] stode on hye the 32
standard of theyr ensygne.   & theyr custome was that
on payne of deth noo persone, shold retorne, ne goo

[1] l vj, col. 2.   [2] l vi, back.   [3] *orig.* thre-vpon.

aback for no thyng as long as the standard stode vpryght.   herof Charles was enformed, wherfore moche
puyssauntly he rode thurgh the sarasyns tyl he came to
4 the standard, and with Joyouse hys swerde he smote it
asondre : and anone as the sarasyns sawe that they
fledde, & mony of ye paynyms were slayn and dede.
& on the morne after the towne was delyuerd vnto
8 Charles by the lord of the toun,[1] whyche coude not
resyste hym, & charles was content to lete hym haue
hys lyf yf he wold be baptysed, and also the toun foto holde it of hym and none otherwyse.   And thenne
12 charles ordeyned in spayne certayn of hys barons to
kepe it, in suche wyse, that none durst assaylle it, ne
make to it warre.   For he was [2]alwaye vyctoryous of
his enemyes by the puyssaunce that he ledde, and also
16 by dyscrecyon of hys persone, and pryncypally by the
grace of god, whyche faylled not in him and in hys
subgettes.

¶ How the chyrche of Saynt Iames was
20   halowed by tharchebysshop Turpyn, & the
   chyrches of spayne subgettes therto, and'
   of other pryncypal chyrches : capitulo xiiij

C Harles the noble emperour, after that he had
24   put and sette good estate and good warde in
spayne, he went to saynt Iames wyth fewe people.
And whan he was there, suche cristen men as he there
fond he rewarded them, & dyd to them moche good,
28 and he punysshed suche as were apostates, & other
maner of peple, suche as he fonde vntryewe and dys-
obeysaunte to holy chyrche, he lete slee and put to deth,
or he sente theym in to fraunce to do penaunce, and
32 bannysshed them.   And thenne thorugh al the cytees
of spayne he ordeyned bysshops, relygyous, and other

Charles himself cuts down the standard, and the Saracens flee.

The town is taken, and all who will not become Christians put to death.

Charles goes to St. James, and makes regulations for the church:

appoints bishops and monasteries,

---
[1] orig. tonn.   [2] l vj, back. col. 2.

Q 2

peple of the chyrche, & made many constytucyons,[1] synodals, and other ordynaunces vp-on the chyrche, and vpon other peple.   And in thonour of saynt [2]Iames he

and ordains that all the bishops of Spain shall be subject to the bishop of St. James.

made constytucyons, and Instytuled that al the bysshops, 4 prynces, and kynges dwellyng in spayne, shold all be subget to the bysshop of saynt Iames, and al they shold owe to that chyrche fydelyte, wyth al the peple of the londe of galyce.   And accordyng to the same the arche- 8 bisshop Turpyn wryteth in thys manere : "And I, Turpyn, archebysshop of Raynes, was in the same place, where the ordenaunces aforesayd were maad.   And I, accompanyed wyth ix honourable bysshops & of good 12 lyf, at the requeste and postulacyon of Charles in the

Turpin consecrates the Church of St. James.

moneth of Iuyl, haue halowed, dedycated, blessyd, and consecrated the chyrche of saynt Iames, & the aulter of the same.   And after thenne the kynge Charles gaf al 16 the londe of spayne & of galyce to that chyrche, And

Charles appoints the payment of tithes to the church,

after ordeyned y[t] euery hous of spayn and galyce shold gyue to the chyrche of saynt Iames iiij pens of the money corraunt for annuel[3] trybute.   And by the 20 moyen therof they shold be franke and free of seruytude.   And for the honour of saynt Iames he establysshed that the chyrche of the sayd place shold be sayd apostolyque for thexaltacion of the place.   And 24

and orders that all consecrations and coronations shall take place there.

more ouer, that the bysshopryches and specyal dygnyte of alle spayne & of galyce, [4]and semblably the coronacions of kynges of al the contre, shold be crowned & sacred by the bysshop of saynt Iames, al in lyke wyse 28 as it hath been tofore doon in Asye in the place of ephesym, for the honour of holy Saynt Iohan theuangelyst, brother of saynt Iames, and sone of Zebedee.   &

The body of St. John is deposited on the right side, and that of St. James on the left.

thus Saynt Iohan was lodged in the ryght syde, And 32 Saynt Iames, hys brother, in the lyfte syde.   Thenne was accomplisshed the peticyon of their moder and of

---

[1] *orig.* constytucyous.   [2] 1 vij.   [3] *orig.* amuel.
[4] 1 vij, col. 2.

hyr two sones, gloryouse frendes of our lord Ihesu
Cryst, whan she desyred that hyr two sones shold sytte,
one on the ryght syde, and that other on the lyfte,
4 whyche was thenne accomplysshed and termyned. &
therfore in the world ben thre syeges and chyrches
pryncypal, whyche crysten men by ryght owen texalte,
deffende and mayntene wyth all theyr myght. ¶ That
8 is to wete, the chyrche of Rome, The chyrche of Ephesym of saynt Iohan the euangelyst, And the chyrche of
Saynt Iames in galyce. And yf ony demaunded the
cause of these thre places and syeges pryncipal of cris-
12 tyente, the cause is ynough apparente. These thre
places ben honoured pryncypally by cause the synners
may haue theyr recours to them for tamende theyr
lyues, and put ¹awaye theyr synnes, & obteyne pardon
16 and forgyuenes. Fyrst these iij appostles, that is to say,
Saynt Peter, Saynt Johan, & saynt James, haue pre-
ceded all the other in the companye of Jhesu Cryst
whan he was in thys world, & haue ben called to hys
20 secretes, and that haue moost contynued wyth hym.
Thus by good ryght, the places in whyche they haue
conuersed and contynued theyr lyues, and where theyr
bodyes resten, oughten to be honoured and to be
24 habundaunt in grace. ¶ Pryncypally, saynt Peter was
the fyrst and moost hye, & preched at Rome, and there
was martred & buryed; Therfor the chyrche of Rome
is enhaunced & exalted aboue al other chyrches. &
28 after saynt Johan, whyche sawe the secretes of god in
his souper, & in ephesym he made the gospel 'In
principio erat verbum & cetera,' And by his holy
prechyng hath conuerted thynfydellys to the holy
32 crysten fayth. And also saynt James, whyche had
grete payne in spayne and in galyce, for the honour of
god as wel for hys holy lyf, for hys myracles, as for hys
marterdom and hys sepulture, by good ryght ought the
memorye of them to be thorugh the vnyuersal world."

¹ l vij, back.

Thus the three
chief churches in
the world are
those of Rome,
Ephesus,
and St. James,

because St. Peter,
St. John, and St.
James were the
chief of the
Apostles.

The church of
Rome is the head,
because there St.
Peter is buried.

Ephesus is next,
because there St.
John wrote his
Gospel,

and the church of
St. James is third.

[1]¶ The second' parte of the thyrd book conteyneth x chapytres, & speketh of the
treason made by ganellon, and' of the deth
of the pyeres of Fraunce.   4

¶ How the treason was comprysed' by Ganellon, and of the deth of crysten men, &
how ganellon is repreuyd by thauctour :
capitulo   primo 8

I N this tyme were in Cezarye two kynges sarasyns
moche myghty, that one was named' marfurrius, and'
that other bellegandus, his brother, whyche were
sente by thadmyral of babylonne in to spayne, the 12
whyche were vnder kynge Charles, & made to hym synge
of loue and' of subgectyon, and went by hys commaunde-
ment holyly and vnder the shadowe of decepcyon.
Themperour, seyng that they were not crysten, and for 16
to gete seygnourye ouer them, he sente for ganellon, in
whome he had' fyaunce, that they shold' doo baptyse
them, or ellys that they shold' sende to hym trybute in
sygne of fydelyte of their contre. Ganellon, the traytre, 20
went thyder and' dyd' to them the message, and' after
that he had with them many deceyuable wordes, they
sente hym ageyn to charles wyth xxx hors laden with
gold & syluer, wyth clothes of sylke, [2]and' other 24
rychesses, & iiij hondred hors laden with swetewyn,
for to gyue to the men of Warre for to drynke ; & also
they sente, aboue thys, to them a thousand' fayr wymmen
sarasyns, in grete poynte and' yonge of age : And al thys 28
in sygne of loue and of obeyssaunce. and after they
gaf to ganellon xx hors charged' wyth gold' and syluer,
sylkes, and other precyosytees, that by hys moyen he
shold' brynge in to theyr hondes the companye of 32
charles yf he myght doo it.

Marginal notes:

Marsurius and Bellegandus, kings of Saragossa, pretend to be ready to submit to Charles.

Charles sends Ganelon, requiring them to be baptized and pay tribute.

The Saracens send presents to Charles, and induce Ganelon, by

bribes, to promise to betray the French army.

[1] 1 vij, back, col. 2.   [2] 1 viij.

Thenne ganellon was surprysed wyth thys fals
auaryce, whych consumeth alle the swetenes of charyte
that is in persones, for to haue gold or syluer & other
4 rychesses, & made a pacte and couenaunte wyth the
sarasyns for to betraye hys lord, hys neyghbours, &
crysten brethern, & sware that he wold not faylle them
of thenterpryse ; but I merueylle moche of ganellon,
8 which made thys treason, wythoute to haue ¹ cause
coloured ne Juste.

¶ O wycked Ganellon, thou were comen of noblesse,
& thou hast doon a werke vylaynnous : thou were ryche
12 & a grete lord, and for money thou hast betrayed thy
mayster.   Emonge alle other thou were chosen for to
goo to yᵉ sarasyns for grete trust : emonge al the other,
and for the fydelyte that was thought in ²the, thou
16 hast consented to trayson, and allone hast commysed
Infydelyte.   Fro whens cometh thyn Inyquyte, but of
a fals wylle plunged in thabysme of auaryce ?   Thy
naturel souerayn lord, Roulland, Olyuer, & the other,
20 what haue they doon to the ?   yf thou haue a wycked
hate ayenst one persone, wherfore consentest thou to
destroye thynnocentes ?   was there noo persone that thou
louedest whan to al crysten men thou hast ben traytre ?
24 was there ony reason in the, whan thou hast ben capy-
tayn ayenst the fayth ?   what auayleth the prowesse that
thou hast made in tyme passed, whan thyn ende shew-
eth that thou hast doo wyckednes ?   O fals auaryce, and
28 ardeur of concupiscence !   he is not the fyrst that by the
is comen to myscheyf.   by the Adam was to god dys-
obeysaunt, and the noble cyte of Troye the graunde put
to vttre ruyne and destructyon.   Thus in thys manere
32 ganellon brought gold and syluer, wyn, wymmen, and
other rychesses, as tofore he had enterprysed.   Whan
charles sawe al this, he thought that al way doon in
good entent and equyte and wythout barat.   The grete

Ganelon bargains
to betray Charles
and his fellow-
countrymen.

The author's re-
proach to Ganelon
for his treachery,

for which he had
no reason but
avarice,

which had ruined
so many.

Ganelon presents
the presents to
Charles,

who falls into the
trap.

---

¹ *orig.* hane.   ² l viij, col. 2.

lordes & knyghtes toke the wyn for them, and charles took onely the gold and syluer, & the moyen people took the hethen wymmen. Themperour [1]gaf consente to the wordes of ganellon, For he spake moche wysely, 4 and wrought in suche wyse that charles and alle hys

hoost passed the porte of Cezarye; for ganellon dyd hym to vnderstonde that the kynges aforesayd wold become crysten and be baptysed, and swere fydelyte to 8 the emperour; And anone sent his peple tofore, and he came after in the ryere warde, & had sente Roulland & Olyuer & the moost specyal of hys subgettes wyth a thousand fyghtyng men, and were in Rouncyuale. 12

Thenne the kynges Marfuryus & Bellegandus, after the counceyl of ganellon, wyth fyfty thousand sarasyns were hydde in a wode, abydyng & awaytyng the frenssh men, & there they abode ij dayes and two nyghtys, & 16 deuyded theyr men in two partyes. In the first they put xx M sarasynz, and in that other they put xxx thousand sarasyns. ¶ In the vaunte garde of charles

were xx thousand crysten men, whyche anone were 20 assaylled wyth xx thousand sarasyns, and maad warre in suche wyse that they were constrayned to withdrawe

them; For fro the mornyng vnto the houre of tyerce they seaced not to fyght and smyte on them, wherfore 24 the crysten men were moche wery, and had nede to reste theym. Neuertheles, they [2]dronken wel of the good swete wyn of the sarasyns moche largely, And

after many of them that were dronke went & laye by 28 the wymmen sarasynoys, & also wyth other that they had brought oute of fraunce, wherfore the wylle of god was that they shold al be dede, to thende that their martyrdom & passyon myght be the cause of theyr 32

saucyon & purgyng of their synne. For anone after the thyrty thousand sarasyns cam that were in the second batayl vpon the frenssh men soo Impetuovsly

[1] l viij, back.   [2] l viij, back, col. 2.

that they were al dede and slayn, Except Roulland,
bauldouyn, & Thyerry. The other were slayn and dede
with speres: somme slayn, somme rosted, and other
4 quartred, and submysed to many tormentes. And whan
thys dyscomfyture was doon, Ganellon was with charles,
and also tharchebysshop Turpyn, whych knewe nothyng
of this werke so sorouful, sauf onely the traytre, whyche
8 supposed that they alle had be destroyed and put to
deth. ¶ Of the languysshe that was comynge to Charles,
he wyste not, how sone it was comyng.

and slay all except
Roland, Thierry,
and Baldwin.

¶ Of the deth of kyng Marfurius, and' how
12   Roulland' was hurt wyth foure speres mortally after that al his peple were slayn :
capitulo :   ij

[1] THe batayle, as I haue sayd tofore, was moche
16   sharpe. whan Rolland, whyche was moche wery,
retorned he recountred in hys waye a sarasyn
moche fyers & blacke as boylled pytche, and anone he
took hym at thentre of a wode & bonde hym to a
20 tree straytely, wythoute doyng to hym ony more harme,
and after took and rode vpon an hylle for to see the
hoost of the sarasyns, And the crysten men that were
fledde : & saw grete quantyte of paynyms. Wherfore
24 anone he sowned and blewe his horne of yuorye moche
lowde. And wyth that noyse cam to hym an hundred
crysten men wel arayed and habylled wythoute moo.
And whan they were come to hym he retorned to the
28 sarasyn that was bounde to the tree, And Roulland
helde hys swerd ouer hym, sayeng that he shold deye,
yf he shewed to hym not clerely the kyng Marfuryus,
& yf he so wold do he shold not deye. The sarasyn
32 was contente, and sware, that he shold gladly do it for
to saue his lyf; & soo he brought hym wyth hym vnto

Roland captures
a Saracen,
whom he ties to
a tree,

and afterwards
compels to point
out to him Mar-
surius.

[1] in j.

Tho Saracen
points out Mar-
surius,
the place where they sawe the paynyms, and shewed to
Rolland Whyche was the kyng, whyche rode vpon a
rede hors, & other certeyn tokenes. And in thys poynt
Roulland, reconfermed in hys strengthe, trustyng 4
¹veryly in the myght of god and in the name of Ihesus,
as a lyon entred in to the bataylle, & emonge them he
encountred a sarasyn whyche was gretter than ony
of the other, & gaf to hym so grete a stroke wyth 8

whom Roland
kills.
durandal vpon the hede that he clefte hym & hys hors
in two partes, that the one parte went on one syde &
that other on the other syde.   wherfore the sarasyns
were soo troubled and abasshed of the myght and puys- 12

The Saracens fly
before him.
saunce of Rolland, that they alle fledde tofore hym, &
thenne abode the kynge Marfuryus wyth a fewe folke.
Thenne rolland sawe thys kyng, And wythoute fere came
to hym and put hym to deth Incontynent.   And alle 16

All the French
are killed, except
three.
the hondred crysten men that were wyth Roulland in
thys recountre were dolorously slayn & put to deth,
Except onely baulduyn and Thyerry, whyche for fere
fledde in to the wode.   But after that Rolland had 20
slayn kyng Marfuryus he was sore oppressyd, & in
suche wyse detoyned that wyth foure grete speres he
was smyton and wounded mortally, & beten with
stoones, and hurte wyth dartes and other shotte mor- 24
tally.   And not withstondyng these greuous hurte &
woundes, yet, maulgre al the sarasyns, he sprange out
of the bataylle, and saued hym self the best wyse he

Bellegandus and
his men fly.
myght.   ²Bellegandus, broder of Marfuryus, doubtyng 28
that helpe & ayde shold come to the crysten people,
retorned in to another contreye³, wyth hys peple moche
hastely.   And themperour Charles had thenne passed
the montayne of Roncyuale, and knewe nothyng of 32
these thynges afore sayd, ne what had be doon.

¹ m j, col. 2.   ² m j, back.   ³ *orig.* coutreye.

¶ How Rolland deyed' holyly, after many mar-
tyres & orysons made to god ful deuoutely,
& of the complaynte maad' for hys swerde
4 durandal : capitulo   iij

ROlland the valyaunt, and champyon of the crysten
fayth, was moche sorouful of the crysten men, by
cause they had' noo socours ; he was moche wery, *Roland, although greatly exhausted*
8 gretely abasshed, & moche affebled' in hys persone, for *by loss of blood,*
he had lost moche of his blode by his foure mortal
woundes, of whyche the leste of them was suffysaunt
for hym to haue deyed, and' he had' grete payne to gete
12 hym oute fro the sarasyns for to haue a lytel com-
memoracion of god' tofore or the soule shold' departe
fro his body. so moche he enforced' hym, that he came *struggles nearly to Saragossa,*
to the fote of a montayne, nygh to the porte of Cezarye,
16 and' brought hym self nygh to a rocke ryght by Ron- *where he lies down.*
cyuale, vnder a tree in a fayr medowe. whan he sat
down ¹on the grounde he behelde his swerde, the best
that euer was, named' durandal, whyche is as moche to
20 say as gyuyng an hard stroke, whyche was ryght fayr
& rychely made : the handle was of fyn beryle, shynyng¹ *He looks with grief on Durandal,*
meruallously ; on hye it had' a fayre crosse of gold, in
the which was wryton the name of Ihesus. It was so
24 good' & fyn, that sonner shold' the arme faylle than the
swerde. he took it out of yᵉ shethe & sawe it shyne
moche bryght, and by cause it shold' chaunge his maister
he had moche sorowe in his hert, and wepyng, he sayd *and weeping, bids it farewell.*
28 in thys maner pytously : ¶ "O swerd of valure, the
fayrest that euer was, thou were neuer but fayr, Ne
neuer fonde I the but good' : thou art long¹ by mesure ;
Thou hast be so moche honoured', that alwaye thou
32 barest with the the name of the blessyd' Ihesus, sauyour
of the world', whyche hath endowed' the wyth the power
of god'. who may comprehende thy valure ? Alas !

¹ m j, back, col. 2.

Roland laments
over his sword
Durandal.
who shal haue the after me? who someuer hath the
shal neuer be vaynquysshed, alwaye he shal haue good
fortune. Alas! what shal I more ouer say for the,
good swerde? many sarasyns haue ben destroyed by 4
the; thynfydels and myscreauntes haue ben slayn by
the; the name of god is exalted by the; by the is
made the path of [1]sauement. O, how many tymes
haue I by the auenged thyniurye made to god! O, 8
how many men haue I smyton and cutte a-sondre by
the myddle! O, my swerde, whyche hast ben my com-
fort and my Joye, whych neuer hurtest persone that
myght escape fro deth! O, my swerde, yf ony persone 12
of noo value shold haue the & I knewe it, I shold deye

Determined that
no Saracen shall
ever have it,
for sorowe." After that Rolland had wepte ynough, he
had fere that somme paynym myght fynde it after his
deth, wherfore he concluded [2] in hym self to breke it, 16

tries to break it
on a rock,
and toke it & smote it vpon a rocke wyth alle hys
myght iij tymes wythoute hurtyng ony thynge the

but Durandal
cleaves the rock
without harm to
itself.
swerde, and clefte the rocke to therthe, and coude in no
wyse breke the swerde. Whan he sawe the facyon and 20
coude do nomore therto, he took his horne, whyche was
of yuorye moche rychely made, and sowned & blewe it
moche strongely, to the ende that yf there were ony
crysten men hydde in the wodes or in the waye of 24
theyr retournyng, that they shold come to hym tofore
they wente ony ferther, and to fore he rendred hys

Roland blows his
ivory horn so hard
that it breaks,
sowle. Thenne, seyng that none came, he sowned it
ageyn by soo grete force and vertu, and so Impetuously, 28
that the horne roof a sondre in the myddle, and the

and the veins of
his neck burst.
vaynes of hys necke braken a sondre, and the [3]synewes
of his body stratcheden. And that noys or voys by the
grace of god came to the eeres of Charles, whyche was 32

Charles hears the
horn and recog-
nizes it,
eyght myle fro hym. The Emperour, heeryng the
horne, he knewe wel that Rolland had blowen it, and
wold haue retorned ageyn, but Ganellon, the traytre,

[1] m ij.   [2] *orig.* cencluded.   [3] m ij, col. 2.

whyche knewe wel alle the fayt, dystourned hym, in but Ganelon persuades him that Roland is hunting.
sayeng that Rolland had blowen his horne for somme
wylde beest that he chaced for his playsyr; For ofte
4 tymes he wold blowe hys horne for lytel thynge, and
that he shold not doubte of nothyng. ¶ And thus he
dyd the kynge to vnderstonde that he byleued hym,
and made none other semblaunte. Neuertheles, Rol-
8 land, leyng in thys sorowe, he peased hys woundes also
wel as he myght, and stratched hymself on the grasse Roland stretches himself on the grass.
to the fresshenes for to forgete hys thurst, whyche was
ouer grete.

12 ¶ Here vpon Baulduyn, hys brother, came vnto hym, Baldwin comes to him.
whyche was moche heuy and sorouful for hys brother
Roullandt, whyche was in that necessyte. And anone
Roullandt sayd to hym, "my frende and my brother,
16 I haue so grete thurst that I must nedes deye yf I haue Roland asks for water, but Baldwin can find none,
not drynke to aswage my thurst.

¶ Baulduyn had grete payne in goyng here and there,
and ¹coude fynde no water, and came to hym ageyn &
20 sayde he coude fynde none; and in grete anguysshe he
lepte² on Roullandes hors, and rode for to fetche charles, and rides off to fetch Charles.
For he knewe wel that rolland was nyghe hys deth.
Anone after came to hym Thyerry, duc of Ardayne,
24 whyche wepte vpon Rolland so contynuelly that he myзt
not speke. but with grete payne Rolland confessyd hym Roland confesses himself,
and dysposed hym of hys conscyence. neuertheles, that
same day Rolland had receyued the body of our lord,
28 For the custome was that the subgettes of Charles that
day whyche they shold fyght were confessyd & comuned
wythoute fayllyng by men of the chyrche, which alway
were wyth them. Rolland, whyche knew hys ende by and knowing his end is near,
32 entyer contemplacyon, hys eyen lyfte vp to heuen, &
hys hondes Ioyned, al stratched in the medowe, began
to say thus: "Fayre lord god, my maker, my redemour, commends himself to God,
sone of the gloryous moder of comforte, thou knowest

¹ m ij, back.   ² orig. lefte

myn entency[o]n, thou knowest what I haue doon for
the bounte that is in the. by thy grete mercy of
whyche thou art enuyronned, by the grace whyche in
the haboundeth, by the meryte of thy passyon, holy 4
and bytter, with a good and humble hert I requyre the
y⁺ tofore the ̄thys day my faul-¹tes, synnes, and ygnor-
aunces may be pardouned to me, and take noo regarde
to the trespaces that I haue doon to the ; but beholde 8
that I deye for the, and in the fayth that thou hast
ordeyned. remembre that thou hengest on the tree of
the crosse for the synnars, and so as thou hast redemed
me, I beseche the that I be not loste. Alas ! my maker 12
god omnypotent, wyth good wylle I departed oute of
my contreye for to defende thy name, and for to mayntene crystendom. ¶ Thou knowest that I haue suffred
many anguysshes of hungre, of thurst, of hete, of colde, 16
& many mortal woundes. And day and nyght to the,
my god, I yelde me culpable ; I mystrust not thy mercy.
thou art pyetous ; thou art comen for the synnars ; thou
pardonest marye magdelene and the good theef on the 20
crosse, by cause they retorned vnto the ; they were
synnars as I am ; lyke as they dyd I crye the mercy,
& better yf I coude saye it. thou byheldest how Abra-
ham was obeyssaunt to the of hys sone ysaac, wherfor 24
he ferde moche the better ; byholde me how I am obe-
dyent to the commaundements of the chyrche : I byleue
in the, I loue the aboue all other, I loue my neyghbour.
¶ O good lord, I beseche the to pardoune & forgyue 28
alle theym that thys day ben deed in ²my companye,
& that they may be saued. Also, my maker, I requyre
the to take hede of the pacyence of Job, for which he
was moche the better, that I deye here for thurst, and 32
am allone. I am wounded mortally, and may not helpe
my self, and take in pacyence alle the sorowe that I
suffre, and am therwyth content whan it pleaseth the.

¹ m ij, back, col. 2.   ² m iij.

as al thys is trewe, pardone me, comforte my spyryte,
receyue my soule, and brynge me to reste perdurable."
Whan Rolland had prayed thus, he sette hys handes *Then he crosses his hands on his breast,*
4 on hys body, holdyng hys flesshe, and after sayd thre
tymes, ¶ "Et in carne mea videbo deum saluatorem
meum," and after layed his handes on hys eyen, and
sayd, "Et oculi isti conspecturi sunt, In thys
8 flesshe that I holde I shal see my sauyour, and these
eyen shal beholde hym ;" and after he sayd that he
sawe thynges celestyal, whyche the eyen of mankynde
myght not see, ne the eeres here, ne the hert thynke,
12 the glorye whyche god hath maad redy to them that
loue hym ; and in sayeng, "In manus tuas, domine, *and saying, "Into thy hands I commend my spirit," expires.*
commendo spiritum meum," he layed hys armes vpon
hys body in maner of a crosse, & gaf and rendred hys
16 soule to god the xvj kalendes of Juyl.

[1]¶ Of the vysyon of the deth of Roulland',
and' of the sorowe of Charles, and' how
he complayned' hym pyetously, & other
20   maters : capitulo   iiij

"THe day that Roulland the marter rendred hys *"The day that Roland died, I, Turpin,*
soule vnto god, I, Turpyn, archebysshop of
Raynes, was in the valeye of Rouncyuale, tofore
24 charles the Emperour, and sayd masse for the soules *was celebrating mass before Charles,*
whyche were passed oute of thys world. And as I
was in the secrete of the masse I was rauysshed, and
herde the aungellys of heuen synge and make grete
28 melodye. And I wyst not what it myght be, ne wher-
fore they soo dyd. And as I sawe the aungellys mounte *and in the 'secret' I saw a vision of black spirits passing*
in to heuen on hye, I sawe comyng a grete legyon of *with great noise,*
knyghtes, alle blacke, ageynst me, the whyche bere a
32 praye, wherof they maad grete noyse and desraye.
whan they were tofore me in passyng, I sayd to them

[1] m iij, col. 2.   •

and I asked them who they were, and demaunded who they[1] were, & what they bare. One of tho deuylles answerd & sayd, 'we bere the

and they told me of the deaths of Marsurius and Roland. kyng Marfuryus in to helle, for long a-goon he hath wel deserued it. And Roullnnd, your trompette, wyth 4 Mychel thaungel & many other in his companye, is brouȝt in to Joye perdurable to heuen.' And as the

And I told the vision to Charles, masse was fynysshed I [2]recounted to charles the vysyon whyche I had seen, how thangellys of heuen bare the 8 soule of Roulland in to paradys, & the deuylles bare

and, while I was speaking, came Baldwin, and told us of the slaughter of our men. the soule of a sarasyn in to helle. Thus, as I sayd these wordes, balduyn, whyche rode on Rollandes hors, cam hastely and said to charles how the crysten men 12 were dede & bytrayed, and how Rolland was hurte, and in what estate he had lefte hym. Assone as he had tolde thys, the crye was made thurgh thoost that

And Charles ordered the army to return, euery man shold retorne backe, & there was a grete 16 bruyt. But themperour Charles, to whome thys mater touched at the hert more than to ony other, auaunced

and he himself in front found Roland dead, hym for to goo thyder; and whan he came he fonde Rolland expyred, hys hondes in crosse vpon hys vysage 20 al stratched. And anone Charles fyl doun vpon hym, and began to wepe moche tenderly, smytyng hym on his vysage, rendyng his clothes, & tormented hys body, & myght not speke a grete whyle. whan he was re- 24 torned to hym self by ardeur of dylectyon and excercyte

and he wept and lamented over him bitterly. of sorowe, he sayd in thys wyse : 'O comforte of my body, honour of frenssh men, suerd of Iustyce, spere that myght not bowe, hawberck that myght not be 28 broken, helme of helthe, resemblyng to Iudas[3] macha-beus in prowesse, samblant to sampson [4]in strengthe, & to Absalon in beaulte ! O ryght dere neuew, tayr & wyse, in batayl ryal ! O destroyer of the sarasyns, de- 32 fendour of crysten men, walle of clergye, staffe to wydowes & of poure orphelyns, Releuer of chyrches,

---

[1] *orig.* w hothey.   [2] m iij, back.   [3] *orig.* Indas
[4] m iij, back, col. 2.

tonge of trouthe, Mouthe wythout lesyng, trewe in al
[ugement, prynce of bataylle, conduytour of the freudes
of god, Augmentour of the crysten fayth, & byloued
4 of euery persone! Alas! why haue I brought the in *And he lamented over him as David*
to a straunge contreye? wherfor am I not dede with [1] *over Absalom,*
the? O Roulland, wherfor leuest thou me heuy &
sorouful? helas! caytyf that I am, what shal I doo?
8 Alas! sorouful, whyther shal I goo? I praye to almyghty
god that he conserue the; I requyre thangellis of heuen
that they be in thy companye; I requyre the marters,
of whom thou art of the nombre, y[t] they wyl receuye
12 the in to the Ioye perdurable.   alway I shal remembre
the wepyng, alway I shal fele thy departyng, as dauyd
dyd of natan & of absalon.   Alas! Rolland, thou goost
in to lyf & Ioye perdurable, & leuest me in thys world
16 sorouful.   Thou art in heuen in consolacion, & I am in
wepynges & tribulacions.   Alle the world is euyl content of thy deth, & thangellys hath brou3t the in comforte.'   In thys manere and otherwyse Charles bewept
20 and [2]sorowed his neuew Roulland.   And he made hys *and, after, caused his body to be embalmed.*
tentys to be sette vp there, for to lodge there al that
nyght, & dyd doo make grete fyres and grete lyghtes
for to watche the body of Roulland; & after he dyd
24 do enoynte hys body with myrre & baulme and other
thynges aromatiques, for to conserue the body from euyl
sauour; and his obsequyes were made, & hys entyer-
ment with grete prayers, offrynges, & almesses in grete
28 contemplacion."

¶ How Olyuer was founden slayn, and' of the
  deth of the sarasyns, & of the deth of
  ganellon, whyche was hydous : capitulo v

32 IN the morne erly, charles came where the bataylle
  had been with his peple, and there they fonde the *Next morning the body of Oliver is found,*
  noble Olyuer stratched oute in maner of a crosse,

<hr>

' *orig.* thith.   ² m iiij.

fastened to four stakes, and flayed. whyche was fastned to foure stakes with iiij cordes & sharply bounden, and fro the necke to the nayles or vngles of his feet and handes he was flayn ; he was al to-hewen, and shotte & hurte wyth speres, sharp dartes, 4 quarellys, & arowes, & beten wyth staues; he was al to-faisshed and broken. wherfore the crye of many of the crysten began to renewe for the hydous deth of Olyuer, and of many other. wherfore Charles [1] sware by 8

Charles vows he will never cease till he has avenged the death of his men. god almyghty that he wold neuer cesse tyl that he had founden the sarasyns, & forthwyth he went wyth his hoost & noblesse. and by cause that the paynyms were moche[2] ferre fro them, god shewed a fayr myracle ; 12

By a miracle the day continues till he overtakes the Saracens, and For that same day was prolonged thre dayes longe wythout that the sonne remeued ony thynge. and they fonde the sarasyns by a ryuer named Ebra in Cezarye, whyche rested them, and ete & dranke at theyr ease, 16 wythout doubtyng of ony thyng. and charles & hys

slays 4000 of them. people came vpon them so Impetuously that in a litel whyle there were slayn iiij M sarasyns, and the other fledde & saued them self. Thenne themperour, seyng 20 that he myght goo no ferther, retorned to rouncyuale,

Then Charles enquires who was the traitor. And began tenquyre vpon the fayt of trayson, and who had doon it, & what man. Thenne he was enformed that Ganellon had made it, and that was the comune 24

Thierry accuses Ganelon. oppynyon of them alle. And emonge alle other Thyerry accused and appeled hym of the treason, and that he wold fyght in the quarel. ¶ For Thyerry had knowleche by the sarasyn that rolland had bounden to a tree. 28

Charles appoints a knight to fight for Ganelon. The kyng charles ordeyned a knyght for ganellon, named pynable, to fy3t ayenst thyerry. And whan these ij champyons were in the lystes, [3]anone pynalle

Thierry slays him, was slayne by Thyerry ; and as wel by thys moyen as 32 by other, it appered clerely that ganellon had bytrayed them. wherfore the emperour Charles, wythoute goyng ony ferther, dyd to take iiij grete horses, & made to sytte

[1] m iiij, col. 2.   [2] *orig.* mocbe.   [3] m iiij, back.

on them iiij stronge men, & bonde ganellon to two
horses by his ij handes, and bonde the two feet to the
other ij horses, & made hym to be drawen with the one
4 hors toward ye eest, & that other toward the weste, that
other ayenst the southe, and that other toward the
north.   In this maner eche of the hors drewe forth his
quarter of the body of the parte whyche he was
8 bounden vnto.

and Charles has Ganelon drawn in pieces by horses.

¶ How after the thynges afore sayd' charles
gaf thankynges & preysynges to god &
saynt Denys, & of the constytucions that
12   he made in fraunce : capitulo   vj

WHan thexecucyon was doon of Ganellon and
executed, charles & hys people cam in to the
place where the frensshe men had be slayn, &
16 bygan to knowe theyr parents, frendes, & lordes, for to
bere them in to halowed place.   they caryed somme
vpon theyr horses ; Other salted them wyth salte, for
to mayntene them to brynge them in to theyr controye ;
20 Other buryed them in the same place, & ¹somme bare
theym on their sholdres.   Somme ennoynted them wyth
oylle and myrre, & somme wyth baulme the best wyse
they myght.   Neuertheles, there were two cymytoyres
24 or chircheyerdes, ryght deuoute & pryncypally halowed
emonge the other, whych were sacred and blessyd wyth
vij bysshops.   That one of the cymytoyres was in erles,
and that othe[r] in burdegale.   & Saynt maxymyen of
28 ays, Saynt Trophyn of arles, poule of nerbonne, Saynt
Saturyn of Tholouse, saynt fontyn of poytyers, saynt
Marcel of lymoges, and saynt Eutrope of xayntes had
sacred and halowed them.   In whyche places were
32 buryed the moost party of the frensshe men slayn and
destroyed in rouncyuale.   Themperour dyd do bere

The French army attend to their dead comrades :
some they bury,
others they embalm and take with them.
Two cemeteries are made, one at
Arles, the other at Bordeaux,
where the French dead are buried.

¹ m iiij, back, col. 2.

rolland, the gloryous marter, vpon two mules couerd
wyth clothes of sylke, honourably vnto bloye, & in the
chyrche of saynt Romayn, the whyche he had edefyed
and founded wyth chanonnes reguler, he dyd rychely 4
burye hym, and wyth grete magnyfycence ; & on hye,
ouer his sepulture, he dyd do sette hys swerde, and at
hys feet he dyd do sette his horne of yuorye.   Not
wythstondyng, after, the horne was taken aweye and 8
borne to Saynt Seueryn at bourdeaws.   At bourdeaulx
were buryed olyuer & gaudeboy, ¹kyng of Fryse, Ogyer,
kynge of denmark ; and Crestayn, kyng of bretayne ;
Garyn, duc of Lorayne, and many other.   As for Eafe- 12
rus, kynge of bourdeaulx ; Euglerius, kyng of guyan ;
lambert, kyng of bourges, and galerus reygnaut, with
v M other, charles gaf xij C vnces of siluer of money
that tyme courant, & as moche of talents of gold, & 16
many robes and mete to poure peple, for sauacyon of
their soules.   and al the londe seuen myle aboute he gaf
to the chyrche of saynt Romayn, and maad it subgette
to that relygyon.   And al bloye, wyth thappertenauntes 20
and the see ayenst the sayd terrytorye, he gaf semblably
to the sayd chyrche for charyte & loue of Rolland, and
ordeyned it so for euer.   and on the day of their passyon he ordeyned that in the same place shold euery 24
yere perpetuelly xxx poure men be fedde and clothed
competently, and thyrty messys songen for them that
there were buryed and entyered, and for alle them that
were dede in spayne for the crysten fayth.   In Arles 28
was buryed the counte of lengres ; samson, duc of bourgoyne ; Naymes, duc of bauyere ; Arnold de bellandus,
and Albert bourgoynon, and other fyue knyghtes, wyth
ten thousand other moyen peple.   Constantyn, pro- 32
uoste of ²Rome, was borne to Rome wyth many other
Romayns, and for yᵉ remedye of theyr soules themperour gaf in arles for almesse xij C vnces of syluer

Roland is buried at Blois, at the Church of St. Romain.

Oliver and others are buried at Bordeaux.

Charles gives all the land for seven miles round to the church of St. Romain, for the sake of Roland,

and appoints masses for the dead.

At Arles are buried Samson, Naymes, and others.

Constantine's body is taken to Rome.

¹ m v.   ² m v, col. 2.

and xij talentes of gold, whyche was worth a greto
somme of gold & syluer courant in that tyme.

¶ How Charles wente in to Almayne, where
4   he deyed' holyly, And of hys deth shewed
to Turpyn, and' of hys buryeng' Impery-
ally : capitulo   vij

8   A Fter the thynges afore sayd, Themperour charles
and Turpyn, wyth the other, came and passed by
vyenne ; & there Turpyn tharchebysshop, a moche
holy man, abode, for he was wery and moche febled
of the payne that he had had for the fayth in spayne.
12 and Charles wente to parys, & anone after he assemaled
al the nobles and the moost grettest lordes of hys contreye, for to establyssh certayn ordynaunces, and for to
gyue thankynges to god & to saynt Denys of the vyc-
16 torye that he had obteyned in his tyme vpon the sarasyns, paynyms, & myscreauntes. And after that he
had thanked god and saynt denys, and to his chyrche
fast by parys, lyke as saynt Poule thappostle and saynt
20 Clement the pope had [1] doon in tyme passed, he maad
constytucyon entyere that al the kynges of Fraunce
present & to come shold obeye to the pastour that shold
be for ye tyme of that chyrche, and that neuere kyng
24 shold be crowned wythoute the pastour of that chyrche,
ne the bysshop of parys shold not be receyued at Rome
wythout hys consent & comandement. And he gaf
many rychesses to y^t chirche, & in token that fraunce
28 was gyuen to that chyrche of saynt denys, he ordeyned
that euery possessour in al ye nacyon of fraunce shold
gyue & be bounden to gyue to the chyrche of saynt
denys, for to edefye & augmente it, iiij pens of money
32 courant yerely & perpetuelly, & al they that shold gyue
it wyth a good wylle, yf they were of bonde & serue

Charles goes to
Vienna,

where he leaves
Turpin,

and thence to
Paris.

He ordains that
all kings of France
shall be crowned
at St. Denis,

and all bishops
should be subject
to the priest of
that church.

Also that every
person should pay
to it yearly four
pence,

[1] m v, back.

and any bondmen
who paid this
should be free.
condycion, he wold' they shold be franke & free of condycyon.   And' after anone these thynges ordeyned, he
went & came tofore the body of saynt denys moche

He prays for the
souls of his
soldiers.
deuoutely, & there he prayed the glorious saynt that he 4
wold' praye vnto our lord' Ihesu Cryst, that alle they y'
were dede of the crysten fayth in the tyme that he had'
regned' that they myght be saued', and' that the payne
that they had' taken my3t be to them the crowne of mar- 8
tyrdom in the glorye perdurable ; & in semblable wyse
he prayed' for al them that wold' ¹paye gladly the pens
aforesayd' to his chyrche.   As god' wold', that nyght

St. Denis ap-
pears to him,
folowyng' saynt denys appyered' to hym, & sayd' to 12
hym in thys manere : " O kynge, vnderstonde me,
knowe thou, that I haue made prayer to god, my maker,
& he hath graunted' that alle they that haue been ayenst
the sarasyns with the haue pardon of al theyr trespaces, 16

and declares that
all who pay the
annual pence to
his church, shall
have forgiveness
of their sins.
& that wyllyngly shal paye the penyes for the edefy-
cacyon of my chyrche & augmentyng' the seruyce of
god', they shal haue amendement of lyf and pardon of
theyr synnes."   This vysyon on the morne themperour 20
recounted to hys peple, lyke as he had herd, by cause
they shold wyth a good wylle pay the penyes that he

And this payment
was called the
Frank of St.
Denis,
had ordeyned ; & he that gaf it was called the franke of
saynt denys, by cause that he was free and' quyte of al 24
seruage by the commandement of the kyng.   After
came the custome that that londe whyche was called

whence the coun-
try has its name
of France.
Gallia loste hys name, & was called fraunce, as it is
named' at thys day, & Fraunce is as moche to say as 28
free of al seruage anenst al peple ; and' therfore the
lordes of Fraunce for this cause emonge al crysten men
owen to be honoured' & praysed'.

¹ m v, back, col. 2.

¶ The recapitulacion of alle thys werke, & of
his deth at Acon, & of hys sepulture :
capitulo   viij

4 ¹ THe kyng Charles contynued gloriously his lyf
in vertuouse operacyons, And whan he felte the
declyne of hys lyf he went vnto Acon, where he   *Charles retires to Acon,*
had tofore doon moche good, & enobled a chyrche of
8 our lady the rounde, the whyche he dyd do make, and
gaf therto grete tresour of relyques of bodyes of sayntes,
of gold & syluer, of clothes of sylke, & other precyo-
sytees meruayllous, and there he deyed in the yere of   *where he dies at the age of 72,*
12 hys age lxxij.   & for the magnyfycence of hys werkes
he was called charles the grete ; & he had iij sones   *leaving three sons*
thenne lyuyng, of whom the fyrst was named Charles,
the second Pepyn, & the thyrd Lowys ; & also he had   *and three daughters.*
16 iij doughters, that one was named Rotrudys, that other
berga, & the thyrd gylla.   & whan he knewe that he
myght noo longer lyue, hys sone lowys, whome he had   *His youngest son, Louis, succeeds him.*
ordeyned for specyal loue kyng of guyan, he lefte to
20 hym the mageste Imperyal.   For to knowe the holynes
& the gloryous ende of Charles, & how he was saued in
heuen, and renomed an holyman, The denoute Turpyn,   *Turpin, at Vienna,*
archebysshop of Raynes, sayth in this manere, "I Tur-
24 pyn, archbyshop of Raynes, was in vyenne in the
chyrche tofore thaulter, & was rauysshed in sayeng' the
psalm, 'Deus in adiutoryum² ³meum intende.' I sawe   *sees a vision of devils,*
a companye of blacke peple lyke Ethyopyens, whych
28 were in quantyte Innumerable, whyche went toward
lorayne ; and I sawe one tofore hys felowes, & I demaunded hym whyther al they wente, the whyche,
beyng' constrayned to ansuere, sayd, 'we alle goo to   *who tell him of the death of Charles, and that they mean to have his soul.*
32 Acon to the dethe of Charles, whyche lyeth a-dyeng'.
And we wyl see yf we may haue hys soule for to bere
in to helle to perpetuel dampnacyon.' Thenne I sayd

¹ m vj.   ² *orig.* adintoryum.   ³ m vj, col. 2.

to hym, 'I adiure the by the vertue of the name of our Lord Ihesu cryst that, wythoute fayllyng, after that ye haue doon, that thou retorne by me.'" Anone after,

The devils return, or he coude fynysshe hys psalme, the deuylles cam 4 retournyng ageyn in the same ordre that they wente. "And thenne I sayd to hym that I had spoken to by-fore, 'what haue ye doon there as ye haue been?'

and tell him that St. James pro-duced so many good works done by Charles, that that same deuyl answerd, that 'James of galyce, frende 8 to charles, hath ben moche contrarye to vs, for whan we were redy for to receyue hys soule, and had egally departed his good dedes and his euyl, he brought so many stones & tymbre of chyrches, whyche he had doo 12 make in the name of hym, that his good dedes sur-

they cannot have his soul. mounted moche his euyl dedes, wherfore we myght haue noo thynge ne parte;' & thys sayd, the deuyll [1]vanysshed awaye," & soo he loste hys vysyon. Thus 16 Charles, in the moneth of feueryere, rendred his soule to god holyly. For after that he retorned fro spayn he dyd but languysshe & appayre in hys body toward hys deth; & in hys ende he ordeyned many almesses, & 20 to say many masses & psaulters. And the vysyon that the gloryous archebysshop Turpyn sawe, is sygnyfy-cacion that he whyche maynteneth and edefyeth chyrches in thys present world, that he maketh pre- 24

Charles is buried with great mag-nificence, in a tomb over paracyon of hys syege in heuen. His sepulture was moche honourable emonge al the sepultures of the world, noble and ryche excellently, and so fayr that it myʒt not be amended. and ouer hys tombe was maad an 28 arche of gold & syluer and of precyous stones, com-prysed by grete scyence. & thyder came Leo the pope, accompanyed wyth prynces Romayns, archebysshops, bysshops, Abbottes, Dukes, Erles, and many other 32

which was set a figure of himself, crowned and seated on his throne. lordes, and dyd do make a fayre representacyon of the body of Charles, clad rychely and Imperyally with a fayre crowne of gold sette on his hede, & satte vpon

¹ m vj, back.

a chayer of gold moche fayre and shynyng, and resem-
bled wel a notable Iuge lyuyng. and they sette vpon On his knees were placed the Gospels,
his knees notably the texte of the four gospelles in
4 fayre letters ¹of gold, & wyth the ryȝt hande he helde
the lettre, & in the lyfte hande he helde the ceptre and in his left hand the sceptre.
Imperial, moche ryche ; & by cause the heed shold not
enclyne to eyther syde, hit was vnderset wyth a chayne
8 of gold & susteyned. And the crowne that was on hys
heed raught to the arche, whiche was al aboue wel made,
& the conduytes of the sepulture were replenysshed
with al good odours aromatyques & precyous, and after
12 closed & shette moche subtylly, & honourably kepte,
as it was wel worthy for to be doon.

¶ Thexcusacyon of thauctour.   ix

THis werke, accomplysshed to the playsyr of god This work contains three books, divided into chapters.
16   tofore wryton, conteyneth thre bookes, by the
   chapytres deuyded, as it appereth openly to the
reders, and I haue made them thre, after that I haue
comprysed in the separacyon and deuydyng of the
20 matyer. Of whyche the fyrst book speketh of the be- The first book tells of the beginning of France,
gynnyng of fraunce, and of the fyrst crysten kyng of
fraunce, whyche was named Cloys by the moyen of his
wyf clotildys, in descendyng to kyng Pepyn, fader of
24 themperour Charles, In the honour of whome thys book
is composed for the moost parte ; to the whyche Pepyn
the lygnage of ²kyng Cloys took an ende in successyon
of the Royalme of Fraunce. And the sayd fyrst book
28 sayth, more ouer, how Charles was nourrysshed, of hys and of the youth of Charles.
corpulence, of hys etyng, of hys strengthe, of hys scy-
ence, & other werkes of magnyfycence. The second
book speketh of the bataylle that Olyuer dyd ayenst The second book, of the duel between Oliver and Fierabras.
32 Fyerabras, the meruayllous geaunte, sone of ballant,
Admyral of spayne, a puyssaunt kynge ; & al the fyrst
parte of the second book is attrybuted to noble olyuer,

¹ m vj. back, col. 2.   ² m vij.

and in the honour of hym. After ye shal fynde how
the peres of fraunce were deteyned in Aygremore and
put in surete, & after saued fynably by florypes, the
curtoys doughter of the sayd ballant; And the holy 4
relyques recouured, and other maters of grete mer-

The third book treats of the conquest of Spain by Charles,
uaylles. The iij book speketh how, by reuelacyon of
saynt Iames, charles went and conquerd spayne &
galyce, where as he dyd operacions vertuous, & made 8
constytucyons of sauacyon, wyth many bataylles doon

of the treason of Ganelon,
by hym and hys subgettes ; and fynably of the trayson
of Ganellon, by the whyche the deth of Rolland was
pyetous, the deth of Olyuer dolorouse, and of the other 12
peres of crysten knyghtes slayn & dede. And fynably

and the death of Charles.
the deth of Charles themperour, as tofore is sayd and
wryton. and [1]after that ony persone wyl here or rede
of thys matere, the table made atte begynnyng shal 16
shewe it to hym lyghtly, yf it be hys playsyr to here or
rede of ye werk in thys book composed.

¶ Thennoye of thauctour : ca.   x

AS I haue sayd at the begynnyng of thys present 20
werke, the escryptures and feates somme haue
ben reduced in wrytyng[1] for to be in memorye,

This work I have written to be a good example to all, how to rule their lives.
to the ende that they that haue doon wel, be to vs
ensaumple in ensyewyng[1] and folowyng them, & they 24
that haue doon euyl may be cause to rewle our lyf for
to come to the porte of helthe. For the comune vnderstondyng[1] is more contente to reteyne parables and
examples for the ymagynacion locall, than to symple 28
auctoryte, the whyche is reteyned by vnderstondyng[1],
and also semblably thystoryes spekyng[1] of our lord
Ihesu cryst, of hys myracles, & of his vertuous subgettes, euery man ou3t gladly to here and retenne them. 32

And I have made it at the request
& it is so, that at the requeste of the sayd venerable

[1] m vij, col. 2.

man to fore named, Maister henry bolonnyer, chanonne
of lausanne, I haue been Incyted to translate & reduyse
in prose in to Frensshe the mater tofore reduced.   as

4 moche as toucheth the fyrst & the thyrd ¹book I haue
taken & drawen oute of a book named myrrour hys-
toryal for the moost parte ; & the second book I haue
onely reduced it out of an olde romaunce in frensshe.

8 And without other Informacyon than of the same book,
I haue reduced it in to prose, substancyally wythout
fayllyng, by ordynaunce of chapytres & partyes of the
sayd book, after the mater in the same conteyned.

12 And yf in al thys book I haue mesprysed or spoken
otherwyse than good langage, substancyally ful of good
vnderstondyng to al makers & clerkes, I demaunde
correxyon and amendement, and of the defaultes par-

16 don.   For yf the penne hath wryton euyl, the hert
thought it neuer, but entended to say wel ; & also my
wytte & vnderstondyng, whyche is ryght lytel, can not
vttre ne wryte thys matere withoute errour.   Neuer-

20 theles, who so vnderstondeth wel the lettre shal wel
compryse myn entencyon, by which he shal fynde
nothyng but moyen for to come to saluacyon.   To the
whyche may fynably come alle they that wyllyngly

24 rede, or here, or do thys book to be redde.   Amen.

¶ And by cause I, Wylliam Caxton, was desyred
& requyred by a good and synguler frend of myn,
Maister wylliam dau²beny, one of the tresorers of the

28 Iewellys of the noble & moost crysten kyng, our na-
turel and soucrayn lord, late of noble memorye, kyng
Edward the fourth, on whos soule Ihesu haue mercy,
To reduce al these sayd hystoryes in to our Englysshe

32 tongue, I haue put me in deuoyr to translate thys sayd
book, as ye heretofore may se al a-longe and pl[a]yn,
prayeng alle them that shal rede, see, or here it, to

¹ m vij, back.   ² m vij, back, col. 2.

of Master Bolo-myer, Canon of Lausanne.

The first and third book I have translated from the *Speculum Historiale*, and the second from an old French romance.

I pray all who may find a fault in it to pardon it,

and attribute to my want of learning, not my good will.

And I, William Caxton, have, at

the instance of Sir W. Daubeny,

translated this book into English

And I pray all to

excuse my rude translation, and forgive the faults they may find.

pardon me of thys symple & rude trans[l]acyon and reducyng, bysechyng theym that shal fynde faute to correcte it, & in so doyng they shal deserue thankynges, & I shal praye god for them, who brynge them and me, 4 after this short and transytorye lyf, to euerlastyng

And this work I finished on the 18th June, in the year of our Lord, 1483.

blysse. Amen. the whyche werke was fynysshed in the reducyng of hit in to englysshe, the xviij day of Iuyn, the second yere of kyng Rychard the thyrd, 8 And the yere of our lord MCCCC lxxxv, And enprynted the fyrst day of decembre, the same of our lord, & the fyrst yere of kyng Harry the seuenth.

¶ Explicit per William Caxton.

NOTES.

Page 1, line 12. " hye hystoryes : " Fr. *histoires haultaines.*

p. 1, l. 13. Fr. *lentendement comun est mieulx content a retenir pour la ymaginacion localle, a la quelle il est subzmis.*

p. 1, l. 15. "gladly :" Fr. *volontiers.*

p. 2, l. 9. Fr. *peult estre que je ieusse bien este informe.*

p. 2, l. 11. See *Introduction.*

p. 2, l. 27. The "*Book of the noble Hystoryes of Kynge Arthur and of certeyn of his Knyghtes*, reduced into English by Syr Thomas Malory, Knyght, and by Mr. William Caxton, deuyded into xxi bookes, chapytred and emprynted in the abbey westmestre ;" was printed also in 1485, folio. It is a book of the greatest rarity. There is a perfect copy in Earl Jersey's library, at Osterley Park, and an imperfect one, wanting four leaves, in the library of Earl Spencer. It was reprinted by Wynkyn de Worde in 1498, folio, and an unique copy of this reprint is also in Earl Spencer's library. " *The last Siege and Conqueste of Jherusalem*," which gives the account of Godfrey of Bullogne, appeared in 1481.

p. 16, l. 22. " the people is boystous & furious, &c. : " Fr. *celluy peuple est austere et furieulx, et, que pis est, sans memoire de dieu.*

p. 17, l. 16. "guarysshed and hool :" Fr. *gary.*

p. 17, l. 33. " and wepte—sayd : " Fr. *plourer moult largement en grant pitie va dire,* &c.

p. 18, l. 11. Fr. *Pour quoy toy comme vray dieu et seigneur ie te requiers, comme ie ne desire croire quen toy fermement : par ta haultaine puissance ie demande.*

p. 19, l. 27. [he] : the pronoun is unnecessarily inserted here : throughout the book the subject is constantly omitted in secondary clauses, where the person or thing spoken of is the same as in the principal sentence. See *Sege off Melayne*, l. 27, and note.

p. 19, l. 31. "autentykly :" Fr. *auctentiquement.*

p. 19, l. 32. "frentes :" clearly an error for " fontes : " the Fr. reads, *composer baptitoires couenablement.*

p. 21, l. 23. " put hym self in relygyon : " that is, became a recluse, devoted himself to religion : Fr. *se mist en religion.*

p. 26, l. 11. " cont[r]ye : " Fr. *pais.*

p. 26, l. 24. " wel a poynte : " Fr. *bien a pointe.*

p. 27, l. 4. "as touchyng the pytauuce:" as regards his share at dinner : Fr. *quant a la pitance.*

p. 27, l. 12. "iij hors shoen :" the Fr. original adds, *venans de la forge.*

p. 29, l. 1. "to hym :" we should here insert "he doeth," according to the reading of the French original, *on fait.*

p. 29, l. 12. "frequentek :" constantly studied : Fr. *frequentoit.*

p. 29, l. 26. "moche ample & boystous :" Fr. *moult ample et robuste.*

p. 29, l. 30. "he etc not for the moost parte, &c. :" Fr. *ne mengoit pour le plus que de quatre metz, si non de la venoison rostie.*

p. 32, l. 21. "be enclosed in Iustyce :" Fr. *soies enclos en iustéce.*

p. 33, l. 19. The original French runs : *ilz se vont trouuer en vng grant bois quon ne pouoit passer a mains de deux iours encores a grant paine, et charles le pensoit passer en vng iour.* The meaning evidently is that the wood was so extensive that they could not pass through it in two days, and even then with great difficulty.

p. 34, l. 1. Psalm cxix. 35.

p. 34, l. 15. "after in the same contreye, &c. :" Fr. *depuis sont veus ces oyceaulx.*

p. 34, l. 24. In the original, *Constantynople.*

p. 37, l. 1. "moment." The original reading is *au mouuement quon tira.* The French *mouuement* is evidently a mistake.

p. 37, l. 30. "And it was ordeyned, &c. :" Fr. *il est ordonne que ou moys de iuing a ays la cite tous les ans on deust venir veoir,* &c.

p. 38, l. 23. "after that I shal mowe, &c. :" Fr. *selon que ien pourray concepuoir.*

p. 39, l. 4. "of rome :" orig. *a rome.*

p. 39, l. 9. "adiouste :" add. Fr. *adioindre.* On the word adjust, as representing the two Latin forms *adjuxtare* and *adjustare,* see Dr. Murray's paper in the *Philological Society's Transactions,* 1880.

p. 39, l. 10. "I haue not founde in the book competent :" this, unintelligible in itself, is explained by the original French, which reads, *ou liure competent,* the last word meaning containing.

p. 39, l. 20. See the different lists of the douzeperes, as given in the various romances in my note to *Sir Ferumbras,* l. 259, where the list given as that found in the *Sowdane of Babyloyne* should be read as that of the original French version in the Grenville copy, 10531. The names given in the *Sowdone* will be found in Dr. Hausknecht's Introduction to his edition of that romance, p. xxvii. For the names in *Roland* and *Otuel,* see my edition, note to l. 688.

p. 40, l. 30. Compare *Sir Ferumbras,* l. 78.

p. 41, l. 13. "as euyl and olde :" Fr. *comme mauvais viella·t.*

p. 41, l. 33. "that I be fugytyf :" Fr. *ie soie fugi.*

p. 42, l. 22. "quasi hurt, &c. :" hurt almost to the death.

p. 42, l. 27. These exploits are related in the *Sowdone of Babylone,* pp. 4 *et seq.*

p. 46, l. 19. "cremeur :" in the original the same.

p. 46, l. 20. " as," read [h]as[t] : Fr. *qui as*.

p. 48, l. 14. " At nede a man knoweth hys freude." See the *Gesta Romanorum*, p. 131.

p. 48, l. 20. See note to *Sir Ferumbras*, l. 988.

p. 48, l. 28. " took to hym." The original adds, *qui estoit estachie a dix riches cloux de fin or*.

p. 49, l. 22. " lodgyce : " Fr. *logis*.

p. 50, l. 3. " oute of mesure : " so outrageous in his conduct and language. " At thys houre, &c. : " Fr. *de cette heure ie vous ottroie*.

p. 50, l. 18. " Andrewe : " Fr. *Andrieu*, does not appear again in the present or any other account of the treason at Roncesvalles, so far as I am aware.

p. 50, l. 21. Compare the corresponding passages in *Sir Ferumbras*, ll. 310 *et seq.*, and the notes.

p. 50, l. 33. " secretly : " Fr. *comme entre ses dens*. Cf. *Sir Ferumbras*, 322.

p. 51, l. 24. " the kyng had gyuen to hym hys gloue in sygne of lycence." The usual mode of giving permission to undertake a duel : compare *Roland and Otuel*, l. 1366, and the *Song of Roland*, l. 482, and notes.

p. 51, l. 31. " where shal I become : " what will become of me ? See Prof. Skeat's note to *P. Plowman*, B. v. 651.

p. 52, l. 22. " he setted nought by hym : " took no thought or heed of him.

p. 53, l. 9. " or : " I have corrected the reading in accordance with the original, which has *ou*.

p. 54, l. 18. Compare *Chanson de Roland*, 376. " *Jamais n'iert hum qui encuntre lui vaillet*."

p. 55, l. 26. " thou art departed of a lowe hous : " Fr. *tu es bien de basse main party*.

p. 56, l. 12. " of the rounde table." An addition of the translator.

p. 56, l. 20. " I trowe thou be hurte." Not in the original.

p. 56, l. 27. " flagons : " *barilz* : " botelles " in the *Sowdan*, l. 1185 : " costrel " in *Sir Ferumbras*, l. 510, on which see note and Introd., p. xii ; at p. 60, l. 6, below, they are called " barylles."

p. 57, l. 21. " Termagaunt : " Fr. *Taluagaunt*.

p. 57, l. 30. " goddes : " the reading has been corrected on the authority of the original, which has *dieulx*.

p. 58, l. 28. " lether of arabye : " Fr. *cuir de capadoce*.

p. 59, l. 3. " to the regarde of hys persone : " *i. e.* in comparison with himself.

p. 59, l. 11. ' I suppose : ' *i. e.* I am sure.

p. 59, l. 18. " grabain." The names of Ferumbras' swords are not given in *Sir Ferumbras* or the *Sowdan*, but in the verse *Fierabras* are said to have been Plorance, Baptism, and *Garbain*.

p. 59, l. 23. [" I wyl saye : "] omitted also in the original, but plainly needed.

p. 59, l. 25.   In the verse *Fierabras* the names appear as *Galans, Munificans*, and *Aurisas*.

p. 59, l. 33.   The verse *Fierabras* gives the names of the swords made by Munificans as *Durendal, Musaguine*, and *Courtain*.

p. 60, l. 6.   " barylles." See p. 56, l. 27, and note.

p. 60, l. 8.   " bendedᵉ : " bound, banded : Fr. *bende*.

p. 61, l. 12.   " seen : " *i. e.* seeing, considering.

p. 61, l. 35.   " thou remembrest : " Fr. *tu tauises*, i. e. thou thinkest of.

p. 62, l. 18.   " vtterance : " Fr. *a oultrance*.

p. 62, l. 23.   " at this stroke : " Fr. *a cestuy cop*.

p. 62, l. 34.   " bowedᵉ and entredᵉ : " Fr. *ploiez et entrez*.

p. 63, l. 1.   " tronchonnedᵉ : " Fr. *tronconne*, i. e. broken to pieces.

p. 63, l. 5.   " in a grete whyle : " Fr. *dune grant peece*, i. e. for a great while.

p. 63, l. 12.   " made : " an instance of the omission of the subject pronoun *he* before the verb.   See p. 19, l. 27, and note.

p. 64, l. 4.   " he was bowedᵉ afterwardᵉ : " Fr. *par derriere*.

p. 64, l. 14.   " playe : " the regular technical term for fencing or fighting with swords. Thus the *Catholicon Anglicum* has : " a Bucler plaer, *gladiator ;* a Bucler playnge, *gladiatura*. þᵉ Swerde & yᵉ bucler (bukiller A.) playnge, *gladiatura*." In the *Ancren Riwle*, p. 212, we have the expression "*pleieõ* mid sweordes." See further in my notes in the *Catholicon*.

p. 64, l. 32.   " reioye : " Fr. *resioyr*.

p. 66, ll. 7-32.   Caxton carefully distinguishes between *you* and *ye :* the former never being used for the nominative.

p. 68, l. 21.   " made a lytel course : " ran away a little distance.

p. 68, l. 24.   There is no mention of Oliver's drinking any of the balm in *Sir Ferumbras* or the *Sowdan*. See Dr. Hausknecht's note to the latter, l. 1191.

p. 68, l. 29.   " beyngᵗ nyghe vnto a grete ryuer, &c." See note 1 in Introduction to *Sir Ferumbras*, p. xii.

p. 69, l. 12.   ["he :"] the omission of the subject pronoun frequently causes ambiguity when two persons are spoken of : the [he] here, of course, refers to Oliver's horse.

p. 69, l. 16.   " aboue : " Fr. *oultre*, i. e. out of, away from.

p. 69, l. 20.   For number of chapter given as " viij " read " xiij."

p. 71, l. 11.   " tenestre : " read " terrestre."

p. 71, l. 21.   " Longyus." On the *legend of Longinus*, see Prof. Skeat's notes to *P. Plowman*, C. xxi. 82—90.

p. 71, l. 31.   " thou." Here the singular pronoun is used rightly as in a prayer addressed directly to our Lord : in the previous lines *you* and *ye* were used, as they were not of the character of a prayer.

p. 72, l. 6.   " for hys gloryous medytacyon." In the original French, *par glorieux meditacion*. " Neuertheles : " Fr. *touttefois*.

p. 72, l. 16.   " soo coueytous in smytyng : " Fr. *conuoiteulx et affoibly*.

p. 72, l. 17.   " a-slepe : " *i. e.* numbed. Fr. *endormie*.

p. 72, l. 19. "at vtteraunce : " *a oultrance :* comp. p. 62, l. 18.

p. 73, l. 8. "for to apoynte wyth the : " Fr. *te faire vne pache.*

p. 74, l. 5. "vylete : " Fr. *ville.*

p. 74, l. 12. "matte." In the original the same. See *Sir Ferumbras*, ll. 2506, 2590, and Glossary.

p. 75, l. 20. "whyche he brake and al to-frusshed euyl : " Fr. *cassa et rompi mallement.*

p. 76, l. 5. "and ranne vpon hym : " Fr. *et se coururent.* The succeeding passage is awkwardly expressed in the translation. The original reads : *et fut premierement frappe Oliuer sur son escu par telle fierte, qu'au prez le poinz de Oliuer a mis en pieces son escu,* which is not much better. The *he,* of course, is Ferumbras.

p. 78, l. 16. "enforced : " exerted. Compare *Sir Ferumbras,* 782—
   "Þan Firumbras *enforcede* hym þer to arise vp-on ys fete."

p. 79, l. 18. "a faus dart : " Fr. *ung faulx dart.* Properly a hand-bill. See *Sir Ferumbras,* l. 966, and note—
   "*falsarz an* feþerd dart."
The expression occurs again, p. 81, l. 28, below.

p. 79, l. 20. "crapauld : " Fr. *crapaulx,* a toad.

p. 80, l. 72. "a pynapple tree : " a pine or fir-tree. The *Catholicon Anglicum* gives : "a Pyne tre (A Pyne Appyltre A.) ; *pinus (pinum fructus eius* A.)." *Apple* was the ordinary word for the cones of the pine or fir. Lyte, Dodoens, p. 769, speaking of the pine, says : "his fruite is great Boulleans or bawles of a browne chesnut colour, and are called *pine-apples.*" See other instances in my note in the *Catholicon.*

p. 81, l. 12. "by force of shotte and of strokes." Altered on the authority of the original, which reads : "*a force de coup et de trais.*"

p. 81, l. 28. "faus dartes." See p. 79, l. 18, and note.

p. 82, l. 6. "it is good to wete : " this does not at all convey the meaning of the original, which runs : *sans le dire se peult entendre.*

p. 82, l. 15. The omission of the pronoun before makyng makes the sentence rather awkward.

p. 82, l. 27. "Amanedys : " Fr. *Amandis.*

p. 82, l. 35. In the *Sowdone* it is Roland and Oliver that are captured : see Dr. Hausknecht's note to l. 1433.

p. 83, l. 9. "wente doun of a mountayn." In *Sir Ferumbras,* 984 :
   "at aualyng of an hulle."

p. 83, l. 20. "morfounded : " Fr. *morfondus,* lit. chilled, affected by cold.

p. 84, l. 31. "ones : " at some time or other.

p. 85, l. 10. "Turpyn." For an account of this celebrated Knight-Bishop, see Dr. Hausknecht's note to the *Sowdone,* l. 1711.

p. 85, l. 19. "sercheden : " compare *Sir Ferumbras,* l. 1093-4.
   "is wounde to *enserche* and saye.
   At is heste þey wente þer-to & softe gunne *taste* is wounde."

p. 86, l. 3. "ballant thadmyral." Laban in the *Sowdone* throughout.

p. 86, l. 32. "sythe." By using this word to render the original *puis*, Caxton has made the whole sentence almost unintelligible.   It should run : " O brullant of mommyere, what is betyd of the noble kyng of Cordube and of my neuewe bruchart, and also of my sone fycrabras, the ledar and captayn of all ? "

p. 87, l. 6. " knyght :" Fr. *damoiseau.*

p. 87, l. 15. In the *Sowdone* the French knights tell their true names.

p. 87, l. 30. " yeman :" Fr. *vassal.*

p. 88, l. 10. " brullant : " in the *Sowdone,* 1512, it is Floripas who advises her father to imprison the Frenchmen, not to slay them.

p. 89, l. 3. " strayt : " Fr. *estroite.*

p. 89, l. 6. See note to p. 79, l. 20.

p. 89, l. 29. " put vnder by fals fortune : " Fr. *soubmis a faulx fortune.*

p. 89, l. 31. " what I make " : Fr. *que ie fays,* i. e. what I am doing, how I fare.

p. 90, l. 11. Compare the description of Floripas as given in *Sir Ferumbras,* l. 5789, *et seq.*

p. 90, l. 28. " whyche was made of one of the fayrye : " Fr. *faicte dune fae.*

p. 91, l. 1. Caxton's translation of Raoul Lefevre's *Jason* was printed in 1477 (Blades).   Several copies are still in existence.

p. 91, l. 11. " doughter : " Fr. *la fille.*

p. 91, l. 26. " Anone florypes had enuye to here hym speke : " Fr. *eult enuie les oyr parler,* i. e. had a great desire to hear them speak.

p. 91, l. 31. " dyshoneste : " Fr. *inhonnestete.*

p. 91, l. 32. " on that other syde : " *i. e.* on the other hand, again.

p. 92, l. 21. " charlemayns : " evidently a misprint for " charlemayne," and not a genitive case.

p. 92, l. 35. " for to meddle wyth : " Fr. *pour vous mesler* = to engage.

p. 93, l. 3. " wel ferre for to be oute : " *i. e.* very far from being out. Perhaps we should read " wel ferre *fro* to be oute."

p. 93, l. 18. " ye can wel playe with maydens, &c."   Compare the corresponding passage in *Sir Ferumbras,* l. 1303, and Dr. Hausknecht's note to the *Sowdone,* l. 1723.

p. 93, l. 29. " a corde & a staffe."   In *Sir Ferumbras,* 1308, Floripas sends for " anuylt, tange, & slegge."   The *Sowdan* agrees with Caxton, for in l. 1647 we are told that she

" a rope to hem lete down goon
That aboven was teyde faste."

p. 94, l. 13. " a gardyn pretoyre : " Fr. *avoit ung pretoire,* i. e. an enclosed yard or space.

p. 94, l. 27. " camuse : " flat-nosed.   See note to *Sir Ferumbras,* 4437, and Glossary.

p. 94, l. 35. " varlet : " a repetition of the original French word.

p. 95, l. 27. " ye be here in surete as ferre as no man hath herde vs." This hardly conveys the meaning of the original, which runs : *se dauenture quelque,* i. e. so long as, or, provided that no man hath heard us.

p. 95, l. 28. "I am not in doubte :" Fr. *en aultre doubte,* i. e. fear.

p. 96, l. 5. "when my fader the admyral destroyed Rome." See my Introduction to *Sir Ferumbras,* p. xii, and Dr. Hausknecht's edition of the *Sowdan,* Introd.

p. 96, l. 6. "lucafar :" in the French versions of the romance *Lucifer* throughout.

p. 97, l. 1. "damage :" Fr. *dommaige.*

p. 97, l. 4. The French reads : *et plusieurs aultres terriennes victoires.*

p. 97, l. 6. "deteyned :" Fr. *detenu.*

p. 97, l. 30. "Rolland." In the *Sowdone,* l. 1668, it is Guy whom Charles orders first to go on the message to Balan. See *Introduction,* and Dr. Hausknecht's note to l. 1665.

p. 98, l. 33. "cosyn." Guy was Charles's nephew : see *Sir Ferumbras,* 1922, 2091, &c., and see Dr. Hausknecht's note to the *Sowdone,* l. 1888.

p. 99, l. 7. "lese :" destroy. Fr. *perdre.*

p. 101, l. 15. "and :" if.

p. 102, l. 5. Comparing p. 183, l. 32, it is clear that we should read "he behelde." On Durandal, see note to *Sir Ferumbras,* l. 988, and the *Sowdone,* l. 875.

p. 102, l. 7. "descerkled :" cut off the circle or band of gold worn round the helmet. Compare *Sir Ferumbras,* l. 622, and note, and the corresponding passage in the *Sowdone,* l. 1182, and Dr. Hausknecht's note.

p. 103, l. 29. "Ogyer :" in *Sir Ferumbras* it is Richard of Normandy who gives the account of Mantrible, which he was able to do, because, as we learn, "he knew all the cost."

p. 105, l. 7. "he hath quytte his contreye of fals peple." There can be little doubt that we should read "he hath not quytte."

p. 107, l. 14. "Naymes": in *Sir Ferumbras,* Roland : the *Sowdone* agrees with our text, see l. 1821.

p. 108, l. 23. "with his berde florysshed." Compare *Roland and Otuel,* 82 ; where Naymes, describing Charles, says :

> " He sittes his duspers Imange,
> With white berde large and lange
> Faire of flesche & felle.
> With a floreschede thonwange,
> Oure noble kynge þat es so strange,
> His doghety men imelle."

p. 113, l. 25. "enterbraced eche other & kyssed :" Fr. *se font baisser et accoller.*

p. 116, l. 27. "gloutons." Cf. *Sir Ferumbras,* 1634, 3841, &c.

p. 118, l. 26. Compare the account of the game "at the coal," given in the *Sowdone,* ll. 1999—2003. In it Lucifer burns the beard of Naymes, who at once kills him.

p. 119, l. 8. "thou wendest to haue made me to muse in thy folyes :" Fr. *tu me cuidas il na pas gaires bon faite muser en tes folies.*

p. 119, l. 17. "no more chargo to playo :" Fr. *na plus cure de ioeur.*

p. 120, l. 7. "put you in poynte :" Fr. *mis en point* = arm yourselves completely.

p. 120, l. 28. "whyche was wel appoynted, &c. :" Fr. *trestien appareille tantost fut par terre verse.*

p. 121, p. 18. Fr. *tousiours a la cue dung viel chien vous tenez.*

p. 122, l. 23. "Marpyn :" in the *Sowdone*, Mapyne ; in *Sir Ferumbras*, l. 2387, Maubyn.

p. 123, l. 23. "he came so wel to poynte, &c. :" slightly different in the French, *il vient la bien a point, car le larron.*

p. 124, l. 29. "hyr spouse that shold be :" Fr. *son espoux advenir.* Compare p. 134, l. 27.

p. 128, l. 11. "doubted :" feared. Fr. *redoubte.*

p. 129, l. 13. "wente in theyr repayre :" went on their way back. Fr. *alloient en leur repaire.*

p. 130, l. 18. "lefte not for to be forthwith quartred, &c. :" he did not hesitate, though he should be at once cut to pieces. In the French, *et pour estre esquartelle presentement il ne se fust tenu quil ne prist celluy sarrazin.*

p. 130, l. 23. "whyche wyth theyr feet and handes al to-bete hym in suche wyse, &c. :" Fr. *que des pies que des mains ilz le vont tant battre* = both with hands and feet they beat him, &c. Compare the corresponding passage in *Syr Ferumbras*, p. 90, l. 2790, and note.

p. 133, l. 19. "so hardy and oute of mesure :" Fr. *si hardis et desmesurez.*

p. 134, l. 27. "hir lone and tocomyng husbond :" Fr. *son espouse aduenir.* Compare p. 124, l. 29.

p. 134, l. 31. "Truste ye none other, &c. :" be sure of this only, that if he die I shall leap out of the wyndowe, &c. Fr. *ne vous fies point que sil meurt.*

p. 136, l. 11. "a morel of grete facyon :" Fr. *moreau de grant fasson.*

p. 136, l. 19. "after that he was recoured :" as soon as he had recovered himself. Fr. *aprez quil se fut recouure.*

p. 136, l. 32. "Inconuenyents :" Fr. *inconueniens* = damage.

p. 137, l. 31. "cryed to hym wyth an hye voys, &c. :" Fr. *luy cria a haulte voix quil luy pleust de la venir baisier, en disant que selle viuoit pour la prousse des barons que son pere ladmiral seroit vne ffoys en son dangier.* The whole passage is very obscure, nor does the corresponding line in *Sir Ferumbras* help much to make it any clearer.

p. 142, l. 3. "at vtteraunce :" Fr. *a oultrance* = exceedingly.

p. 142, l. 7. "esmaye you nothyng yet :" Fr. *ne vous esmaies encore.*

p. 142, l. 12. "beurage :" Fr. *beuuraige,* a draught.

p. 142, l. 30. "For they sawe parte of the walles, &c. :" Fr. *car ilz veoient a terre ruer les murailles principalles du chasteau.*

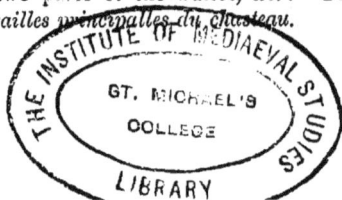

p. 143, l. 25. "be ye .. ne wroth ayenst Mahon :" in the *Sowdone* Balan smashes Mahound.

p. 144, l. 15. "the frensche men purpose to dystrouble vs at our souper :" Fr. *les francoys nous veullent faire refrodier notre soupper* = wish to make our supper cold.

p. 145, l. 1. "wherfor of veray force the other paynyms must retorne :" Fr. *pourquoy force fut aux aultres*, &c.

p. 145, l. 25. "sythe he is a man of auctoryte :" Fr. *puis quil est homme de audience*.

p. 147, l. 5. "abandonned hym self to goo :" offered himself, volunteered.

p. 147, l. 26. "greued in hys persone :" wounded. Fr. *greue de sa personne*.

p. 149, l. 5. "on a day emonge al other :" Fr. *ung iour entre les aultres*.

p. 149, l. 17. "at al aduenture :" Fr. *a son aduenture*.

p. 149, l. 28. "he doubted entyerly :" Fr. *il doubta entierement* = feared greatly, or in his heart. See *Glossary*.

p. 151, l. 6. "dropped :" Fr. *platz* = broad.

p. 152, l. 6. "attayned ouerthwart the necke :" Fr. *lattaint du trauers du col*.

p. 154, l. 4. "of thy partye :" = so far as thou art concerned. Fr. *de ta part*.

p. 154, l. 13. Fr. *Et quant ladmiral les vit venir tout ethroclite en son entendement*. I can make nothing of "the ethroclytes."

p. 155, l. 8. "Orages :" in *Sir Ferumbras*, 3823, Malyngras ; in the *Sowdone*, 2145, Espyard.

p. 155, l. 29. "To whom there is none like or equal in goodness in the world :" Fr. *quil non y a point de pareil*.

p. 158, l. 2. "in comyng, &c. :" as we should now see, *en passant*, or by the way. Fr. *en venant vous debuez scauoir*.

p. 158, l. 5. The miracle of the water rising to a level with the banks, and afterwards subsiding, is not given in the English metrical versions of the romance. See Dr. Hausknecht's note to the *Sowdone*, l. 2810.

p. 159, l. 10. "dantesuyle." In the original French, *dautefuille*, evidently misread by Caxton.

p. 161, l. 1. "how am I determyned :" Fr. *comme suis ie determiné*.

p. 161, l. 29. "as a theef attaynt :" Fr. *comme larron prouue*.

p. 163, l. 12. "deffende :" forbid. Fr. *ne plaise pas a dieu que iamais*.

p. 165, l. 31. "wyth motye :" Fr. *a ce mouuement vous viendrez*.

p. 167, l. 14. "reclame me recreaunte, &c. :" Fr. *reclame recreant et tenu reboute*.

p. 169, l. 3. "bowed his hede :" Fr. *baissa le menton*.

p. 169, l. 28. "of an olde Serpente, &c. :" Fr. *dung viel serpent crote et moult endurcy*.

p. 170, l. 27. "confanon :" so in the original French.

p. 171, l. 27. "she was departed fro her gesyne, &c. : " Fr. *qui auoit faicte sa gessine de deux filz,* that is, who had given birth to two sons.

p. 172, l. 11. "facyon : " = state of affairs.

p. 175, l. 24. "Thus doyng : " = while this was happening.

p. 175, l. 32. "Amyotte." Amyote, *Sir Ferumbras,* 4663 ; Barrok, in the *Sowdone,* 2939.

p. 177, l. 10. In the *Sowdone,* 3043, Richard is left as governor of Mantrible.

p. 177, l. 35. "he swowned, &c. : " Fr. *il pasma de dueil et cria comme tout hors du sens.*

p. 178, l. 11. "wel abused : " Fr. *bien abusez* = greatly deceived or mistaken. This is almost the oldest use of the word. "*Abuser.* To abuse, misuse . . . deceive, disappoint, gull, cozen, beguile. *S'abuser.* To mistake, to be in error ; to wronge himselfe, &c." Cotgrave.

p. 179, l. 7. "the olde kyng Coldroe tempested hym." Here Caxton has made a most curious mistake. The original runs : *et auec luy le viel roy Coldroe, tempeste, et brullant de mommiere : tempeste* being really the name of one of the Saracen kings, and not a verb.

p. 183, l. 5. "better aduysed : " Fr. *quil soit desensle(?).*

p. 183, l. 32. "byhelde : " Fr. *regarderent.* See note to p. 102, l. 6.

p. 184, l. 13. "Duc Naymes." In the *Sowdone* Floripas first sees the French army advancing.

p. 187, l. 1. "in the tree of the crosse : " Fr. *en larbre.*

p. 187, l. 14. "he was almoost in a rage of hys wordes : " Fr. *a peu de fait quil ne fut enraige de ses parolles.*

p. 187, l. 33. "by presumyng : " Fr. *par presumacion* = by supposition.

p. 190, l. 2. "wythoute faulte : " Fr. *sans faulte* = without fail.

p. 193, l. 29. "helde them soo short, &c. : " Fr. *et les tindrent si de prez quelz ne sceurent que faire.*

p. 195, l. 11. "a grete abusyon : " Fr. *grant abusion.*

p. 201, l. 7. "that there was non abusyon, &c. : " Fr. *quil ny auoit point dabusion en croire et adorer les distes reliques.*

p. 202, l. 22. "al rauysshed : " Fr. *tout rauy.*

p. 204, l. 7. "ouerthrew to the erthe : " Fr. *vont tomber par terre.*

p. 208, l. 18. "he founded, rented, and releued many and dyners chyrches : " Fr. *il fonda, renta, et releua plusieurs et diuerses eglises.*

p. 209, l. 4. See Dr. Hausknecht's note to the Sowdon, l. 1888.

p. 209, l. 23. "he wold not leue herby : " would not stop at this. Fr. *ne se voulst tenir a cecy.*

p. 209, l. 27. "maad certeyn experyences : " Fr. *fist aulcunes experimentacions.*

p. 213, l. 5. "took hede : " Fr. *sen prist garde* = took notice.

p. 214, l. 31. Fr. *eulx qui estoient presens et leurs successeurs fussent francs et liberez, les taillables fussent a leurs drois comme quilz fussent condicionez.*

p. 215, l. 35. "felow : " Fr. *compaignon de escoc.*

p. 217, l. 13. "wythoute makyng' grete rebellyon : " without showing any great fight. Fr. *sans faire grandes rebellions.*

p. 221, l. 17. "demaunded syngnler persone ayenst a persone : " Fr. *demanda a Charles bataille singuliere de personne a personne.*

p. 222, l. 17. "soo vylaynsly : " Fr. *si villement.*

p. 231, l. 1. "surprysed : " overcome, taken. Fr. *surpris.*

p. 237, l. 1. "dystourned : " turned him away, dissuaded him. Fr. *le destourba.*

p. 237, l. 21. "lepte : " corrected on the authority of the original French, which reads *monta.*

p. 242, l. 6. "to-faisshed and broken : " Fr. *il estoit naure, casse, et tout rompu.*

p. 251, l. 27. "daubeny." See *Introduction,* p. 7.

GLOSSARY.

Abuse, *s.* 60/30, deceit, error.

Abuse, *v.* 206/19, deceive.

Abylled, *pt. s.* 80/11, dressed, prepared.

Accomplysshe, *v.* 125/34, complete, finish.

Accumyled, *pa. par.* 198/167, accumulated, grown long and thick.

Acoward, *v.* 173/15, show to be a coward, prove oneself a coward.

Adiouste, *v.* 39/9, to add, append.

Adoubed, *pa. par.* 95/22, arrayed, dressed; 55/5, dubbed.

Affectuously, *adv.* 13/12, affectionately, with affection.

Alowed, *pa. par.* 49/20, praised.

Ampull, *s.* 20/31, a flask, a bottle, a jar.

And, *conj.* 101/15, if.

Anenst, *prep.* 246/29, towards, as regards.

Appeled, *pt. s.* 242/26, accused, challenged, charged with.

Araught, *pt. s.* 76/28, reached to, touched.

Arbalastre, *s.* 104/12, a cross-bow.

Aresonned, *pa. par.* 52/20, questioned.

Attayned, *pt. s.* 190/19, reached, struck.

Attones, *adv.* 56/14, at once, at the same time.

Aualed, *pt. s.* 158/16, sank down, was lowered; 104/34, let down, lowered.

Bacynet, *s.* 32/15, a small helmet.

Barat, *s.* 231/35, fraud, deceit.

Baston, *s.* 182/4, a staff.

Batayl, *s.* 232/35, a battalion, a division of an army.

Bayned, *pa. par.* 89/20, bathed, plunged.

Baynes, *s. pl.* 95/20, baths.

Becke, *s.* 20/30, a beak, bill.

Behoeful, *v.* 145/25, advisable, advantageous.

Belfraye, *s.* 175/7, a tower. See *Cath. Anglicum*, s. v. Barsepay.

Blynfelde, *pt. pl.* 82/1, blindfolded. See *Cath. Anglicum*, s. v. Blyndfeyld.

Bowedrau3t, *s.* 189/31, a bowshot.

Boystous, *a.* 29/26, large, big; 16/22, rough, violent.

Broched, *pt. s.* 101/35, spurred.

Buscage, *s.* 33/19, a wood. O.Fr. *boscage.*

Camuse, *a.* 94/27, short, thicknosed.

Chauffed, *pa. par.* 95/20, warmed, heated.

Complyces, *s. pl.* 164/33, accomplices.

Confanon, *s.* 170/27. For gonfanon = a standard.

Confysked, *pa. par.* 24/34, confiscated.

Conuenably, *adv.* 19/32, suitably, fittingly.

Corobere, *v.* 24/9, to strengthen.

Crapauld, *s.* 79/20, a toad.

Cremeur, *s.* 46/19, dread.
"*Cremeur*, fearo, dread." — Cotgrave.

Cresme, *s.* 20/32. The chrism or holy oil with which kings were anointed at their consecration. See *Cath. Anglicum*, s. v. Creme.

Dedyed, *pa. par.* 16/35, dedicated.

Delyuer, *a.* 80/33, active, nimble. Hence the modern *clever*.

Deposshe, *v. imp.* 53/9, hasten, hurry.

Dorked, *pt. s.* 211/12, was eclipsed.

Descerkled, *pt. s.* 102/7, cut off the circle or ring round the helmet.

Descouuerd, *pa. par.* 75/26, uncovered, deprived.

Desmaylled, *pa. par.* 69/10, deprived of the mails or plates.

Disrenge, *v.* 226/19, to be thrown in disorder.

Dyshoneste, *s.* 91/31, filth, nastiness.

Dyssymyled, *pa. par.* 13/22, disguised.

Dystourned, *pt. s.* 237/1, turned aside.

Dystrouble, *v.* 151/27, trouble, disturb, interfere with.

Egal, *s.* 59/2, equal, match.

Empesshed, *pa. par.* 219/14, hindered, obstructed.

Enforced, *pt. s.* 78/16, exerted.

Engyne, *s.* 165/21, craft, art, skill.

Enhardyed, *pt. pl.* 192/22, encouraged, took courage.

Ensyewyng, *v.* 250/24, following.

Enterbraced, *pt. pl.* 113/25, embraced.

Enterprenour, *s.* 166/10, enterpriser, actor.

Entretene, *v.* 46/32, to treat, behave towards.

Entyer, *a.* 237/32, earnest, hearty.

Entyered, *pa. par.* 244/27, interred.

Entyerly, *adv.* 149/28, earnestly, very greatly. "Entyrly: *intime.*"—*Cathol. Anglicum.*

Escrye, *v.* 77/27, to call upon, invoke.

Faus, *a.* 79/18. *See note.*

Faysyble, *a.* 49/34, possible to be done, feasable.

Felounye, *s.* 109/30, daring, recklessness.

Foro, *v.* 140/5, to frighten.

Ferfully, *adv.* 193/32, in fear, timidly.

Fette, *pt. s.* 223/26, fetched.

Fliese, *s.* 91/1, a fleece.

Florysshe, *v.* 36/3, to bud, flower.

Florysshed, *pa. par.* 108/23, flowing, long and wide.

Formosyte, *s.* 198/10, beauty.

Frequented, *pt. s.* 29/12, made frequent use of.

Geayler, *s.* 89/1, jailer.

Glaues, *sb. pl.* 81/27, glaives: weapons made of a cutting blade fixed at the end of a staff.

Gree, *s.* 96/10, pleasure, delight.

Greued, *pa. par.* 147/26, hurt, injured.

Guarysshed, *pa. par.* 17/16, cured, healed.

Habylle, *a.* 169/32, active, nimble.

Harnoys, *s.* 105/34, equipments, outfit.

Houyng, *pr. par.* 36/16, hovering.

Iape, *v.* 60/22, play, mock.

Ionques, *s. pl.* 200/1, rushes. See *Cath. Anglicum*, s. v. Ionkett.

Iourneye, *s.* 216/9, a day's journey.

Lawhe, *v.* 53/12, to laugh.

Lawhyng, *a.* 90/15, laughing.

Lesynges, *s. pl.* 106/8, lies.

Leteth, *pr. s.* 212/24, causes. *Leteth the wete* = tells you, sends notice to you.

Lette, *pa. par.* 219/14, obstructed, hindered.

Loange, *s.* 25/32, praise, worship, reverence. O.Fr. *louange.*

Lodgyce, *s.* 49/22, lodgings, tent. Fr. *logis.*

Loos, *s.* 85/5, glory, praise.

Lyces, *s. pl.* 40/25. Lists or a tilt-yard (*Cotgrave*) here used for the lines of the camp.

Lygnage, *s.* 192/33, clan, party.

Maistresse, *s.* 94/19, governess.

Matte, *a.* 74/12, conquered, throughly beaten. See glossary to *Sir Ferumbras.*

Maulgre, *prep.* 234/26, in spite of.

Moddle, *v.* 92/35, engage, contend.

Medled, *pa. par.* 198/14, mixed, intermingled.

Mesprysed, *pa. par.* 251/12, made a mistake, erred; 52/6, done wrong, injured.

Mosel, *s.* 151/10, a muzzle.

Moyen, *s.* 213/33, a means, a plan.

Murayl, *s.* 203/25, walls, fortifications.

Muse, *v.* 119/9, to be confounded.

Oueral, *adv.* 30/12, everywhere. "Ouer alle; *passim, vbicunque, genus loquendi est vbique.*"—*Cath. Anglicum.*

Ouerthrewe, *pt. s.* 141/18, fell over.

Parents, *s. pl.* 160/3, relations.

Pourchace, *v.* 32/6, provide, contrive. See note to *Sir Ferumbras,* 2603.

Prestly, *adv.* 94/35, readily, quickly.

Priued, *pa. par.* 215/14, withdrawn, estranged.

Purchaced, *pa. par.* 131/8, obtained, procured.

Putayne, *s.* 180/1, a harlot.

Puterye, *s.* 181/35, harlotry. Fr. *puterie.*

Pynapple, *s.* 80/22, a fir. *See note.*

Raught, *pt. s.* 81/18, reached to, touched.

Reioye, *v.* 64/32, renew.

Releued, *pt. s.* 130/24, lifted up, raised.

Remysed, *pt. s.* 208/28, placed again, brought back.

Rented, *pt. s.* 206/18, endowed.

Repayre, *s.* 129/13, retreat, return.

Rescowed, *pa. par.* 72/35, rescued.

Retcheth, *3 pr. s.* 22/3, cares, recks.

Ryuage, *s.* 158/3, shore, bank.

Salowed, *pt. s.* 49/23, saluted, made obeisance to.

Setted, *pt. s.* 52/22, set, thought.

Share, *pt. s.* 76/28, cut.

Sommyers, *s. pl.* 105/23, packhorses.

Soulded, *pa. par.* 103/33, soldered, fastened, jointed.

Sperhawke, *s.* 193/32, a sparrowhawk.

Stratcheden, *pt. pl.* 236/31, were stretched or strained.

Sudarye, *s.* 37/14, a handkerchief: commonly applied to the napkin which wrapped about our Lord's head. See *Cath Anglicum,* s.v. and note.

Surquydrous, *a.* 74/10, proud, haughty.

Swolowe, *s.* 205/32, a whirlpool or quicksand. See *Cath. Anglicum,* s.v. a Swalle of y* See.

Symylacres, *s. pl.* 206/11, images.

Syeges, *s. pl.* 229/5, seats, places.

Tabellyons, *s. pl.* 214/32. *See note.*

Tabouryns, *s. pl.* 22/27, tabourers.

Thwarte, *prep.* 44/6, across.

To-frusshed, *pa. par.* 75/20, broken to pieces.

Trauaylled, *pa. par.* 103/7, worn out with labour.

Tronchonned, *pa. par.* 63/1, broken to pieces.

Truffed, *pt. s.* 119/15, played, mocked.

Tyerce, *s.* 232/23, terce, or the third of tho canonical hours.

Underset, *pa. par.* 249/7, proppod up, supported.

Vnncthe, *adv.* 31/6, scarcely, with difficulty.

Vylaynsly, *adv.* 222/17, shamefully, disgracefully.

Wende, *pt. s.* 36/13, thought, intended.

Wessho, *pt. s.* 66/21, washed.

Wynbrowes, *s. pl.* 26/33, oyebrows. Evidently a corruption of *eyenbrowes.*

Ymbre, *s.* 37/35, ember.

BUNGAY: CLAY AND TAYLOR, PRINTERS, THE CHAUCER PRESS.

www.ingramcontent.com/pod-product-compliance
Lightning Source LLC
Chambersburg PA
CBHW031451270326
41930CB00007B/948